W9-BNQ-956

CALLED TO CARE

Biblical Images for Social Ministry

Robert Kysar

Fortress Press   Minneapolis

To the women and men
who are bearers of God's care in
the social service agencies of
the Northeastern Pennsylvania Synod of
the Evangelical Lutheran Church in America

CALLED TO CARE
Biblical Images for Social Ministry

Copyright © 1991 Augsburg Fortress. All rights reserved. Except for brief quotations in critical articles or reviews, no part of this book may be reproduced in any manner without prior written permission from the publisher. Write to Permissions, Augsburg Fortress, 426 S. Fifth St., Box 1209, Minneapolis, MN 55440.

Scripture quotations unless otherwise noted are from the New Revised Standard Version Bible, copyright © 1989 by the Division of Christian Education of the National Council of the Churches of Christ in the United States of America.

Cover design: Eric Walljasper

Cover art: *The Good Samaritan* by James J. Tissot, gouache on paperboard. From the collection of The Brooklyn Museum, 00.159.175. Published by Public Subscription.

Library of Congress Cataloging-in-Publication Data

Kysar, Robert.
    Called to care : biblical images for social ministry / Robert
Kysar.
      p.   cm.
    Includes bibliographical references and index.
    ISBN 0-8006-2470-X (alk. paper)
    1. Service (Theology)—Biblical teaching. 2. Service (Theology)
3. Church work—Biblical teaching. 4. Church work. 5. Church and
social problems—Biblical teaching. 6. Church and social problems.
I. Title.
BS680.S47K97   1991
253—dc20   90-29312
                                                     CIP

The paper used in this publication meets the minimum requirements of American National Standard for Information Sciences—Permanence of Paper for Printed Library Materials, ANSI Z329.48-1984. ∞™

Manufactured in the U.S.A.

2   3   4   5   6   7   8   9   10

Contents

Preface   ix

Introduction   1

**Part One: Biblical Images for
            Social Ministry**   5
1. Old Testament Images of God   7
2. The Jesus Image of God   31
3. Images of Community and Discipleship   59
4. Images of the Future   79

**Part Two: Practical Directions for
            Social Ministry**   97
5. Changing the Popular Consciousness   99
6. Overcoming the Phobias   121

A Brief Theology of Mission   143

Bibliography   149
Index   155

Preface

As Christian congregations, we are called to care. Only by reviving the biblical understanding of Christian service can the social ministry of the church be fostered. This premise means that other appeals made to support the church's social ministry are inadequate.

The first such appeal is humanitarian. This assumes that Christians are motivated to act on behalf of needy humans by a kind of instinctual sense that so acting is good. This is the general appeal made to the public to support worthy causes of all kinds. I find such appeals inadequate because they evoke little more than minimal support, even among Christians. "Do unto others as you would have them do unto you" may be a prudent bit of wisdom, but the Christian motivation for aiding the needy neighbor is more than long-range self-interest. The church, when offering this appeal, is no more compelling than any of the humanitarian agencies in the world.

The second such appeal is a general duty of kindness for the neighbor. Granted, such an undefined and imprecise concept guides many Christians in their moral lives. But in the long run such an appeal works against any clear intentionality in social service, because it is prone to reaction rather than proaction—to address human needs when it becomes apparent that these are life-threatening, but never concerned to act to prevent the escalation of such needs. Again, such an appeal is less than Christian, because it lacks a clear understanding of what motivates Christians to render service to those in need. A Christian congregation's call to care for societal needs arises from more than a simple duty of kindness.

Congregations and the individual Christians who populate them need more compelling and empowering appeals than either a broad humanitarianism or vague sense of kindness. This book seeks to provide them. First, the church itself needs a foundation in the biblical and theological understanding of the reasons the people of God are called to be about the task of addressing the whole range of human needs in a society. Anything less than this foundation will prove short-lived and frustrating. Second, this biblical mandate for social ministry contains clear practical directions for that ministry. Without the benefit of this biblical foundation and its directions our ministry to social needs will be deficient. Hence, the first four chapters elucidate the reasons for social ministry as these arise out of the witness of Scripture. The last two chapters illustrate how the Bible addresses some practical, congregational concerns surrounding ministry to social needs.

Footnotes are kept to a minimum and are intended to direct reader to materials developed at greater length. The notes are keyed to the bibliography where the full citations are given. I recognize numerous places at which I have not acknowledged my indebtedness to published material and to scholarly research.

The tributaries that have converged to produce the flow of this book are many, some of which will remain undiscoverable. Nevertheless, a number of them must be acknowledged. This work is the culmination of two major streams in my life. On the one hand, I have been preoccupied with the social ministry of the church as long as I can remember. On the other, I have devoted my professional career to the study and teaching of the Bible on behalf of the church. The opportunity to bring these two together in a systematic way was occasioned by my appointment as a teacher and theologian for social ministry in the Northeastern Pennsylvania Synod of the Evangelical Lutheran Church in America. Much of what is contained in the following pages took shape in the course of my work in that capacity. I must, therefore, acknowledge and express my gratitude to those who believe so deeply that the social ministry of the church needs a clear biblical and theological foundation, most especially the Reverend Dr. Leon A. Phillips, Jr.

The five social service agencies of the Northeastern Pennsylvania Synod are in part responsible for arranging a grant in the fall of 1987 which made the writing of a large part of this book possible. I am especially grateful to the chief executive officers of Lutheran Services of Lehigh Valley, the Lutheran Home at Topton, Lutheran Welfare Service, Lutheran Inner Mission Society, and the Good Shepherd Home.

I would be remiss not to acknowledge all that I learned from teaching much of the material in this book. Therefore, thanks are due to the numerous lay and clergy groups who responded to my ideas and enlightened me with their questions and statements. The formal classes on "The Bible and Social Justice" taught at Muhlenberg College and the Lutheran Theological Seminaries in both Gettysburg and Philadelphia were equally helpful, and the students in those classes have my gratitude for all they taught their teacher.

Most important, however, has been the influence of my colleague in ministry and wife, the Reverend Dr. Myrna C. Kysar, who has demonstrated an exemplary passion for social service in her own ministry. As always, her support and encouragement provided the major force that motivated me to produce this work. My hope is that for her, other pastors, seminarians, and laity who seek faithfulness in ministry there may be something in these pages that will clarify the call to care.

Introduction

Pastor Johnson thought she was ready. She had served in this parish for eighteen months now. During that time she had won the trust and respect of many of the parishioners, had come to love them dearly as her Christian family, and had observed that the committees of the congregation had begun to take responsibility for much of the programming in the parish. In addition, she had done her homework on the proposal at hand: the tentative opening of a food pantry to address the increasing problem of poverty in the county, due in no small way to the rise in unemployment occasioned by the closing of the small factory on the edge of town. The ecumenical alliance of pastors in the town had agreed to the task, the pastors had conscientiously planned what would be needed in the way of start-up funds, how the distribution would be done, and what would be required of each participating congregation.

Pastor Johnson had asked that the matter be placed on the agenda for the evening meeting of the Social Ministry Committee. She was armed with statistics, a couple of anecdotal accounts of need, and copies of the carefully prepared proposal of the ministerial alliance. When her turn came on the agenda, she laid the proposal step by step before the group. Then, she asked if there were any questions.

The initial silence did not surprise her. But she was taken back by the first response. "How do we know the food will get to the people who really need it?" She thought that the plan had accounted for that, but she explained it again. As she did so, it occurred to her that it was the word "really" that carried the weight of the question. Then came the stories of the abuse of the food stamp program, followed by the assertions that the poor were often so because they did not properly manage their resources. "Why, you would be surprised at the number of them who have color television sets!" "Is this really the job of the church anyway?" Mr. Anderson asked, implying that all would agree with him that it wasn't. "We would do better to let the county handle this sort of thing and spend our money on new carpeting for the church nave."

From that point on Pastor Johnson knew the issue was doomed, at least for now. (Mr. Anderson was one of those powerful figures in the congregation, whose opinion was seldom challenged.) In spite of her efforts, it seemed that the committee was not ready for a community project of this kind. She retreated into silence, hurt and disappointed that the people she had come to love so much harbored views of the kind she heard expressed around the table.

Driving home that evening, she tried to assess what had gone wrong. Was she too aggressive? Was the plan flawed in some way that she had overlooked? Then the real reason for the reluctance of the committee exploded into her consciousness. It was not her efforts or the plan but the history of the life of the congregation that had blocked the proposal. She was vaguely aware of the fact that the congregation had never had a commitment to community service. There was a great deal of talk about the spiritual mission of the church, but little about its mission to address the physical needs of people, with the possible exception of its own members.

The foundation was faulty. Somewhere this congregation had never been led to build its understanding of itself on the basis of a mission orientation. They were never sensitized to the call to care for others beyond their congregation who suffered need. Pastor Johnson was faced with two alternatives. Either she could fit into this limited vision and conduct a cordial and pastoral ministry that neglected the challenge of mission or she would have to start building a new foundation. At the thought of the latter she sighed. What a task! How do you begin to undo years and years of self-understanding? How do you "jack up" a congregation and replace their foundational sense of their reason for being with a new one?

She knew what she had to do. She knew, too, that there was but one place to start. She had the occasion in the adult Bible class to invite people to see the biblical vision of the community of faith in a new way and to hear the biblical call to care with new ears. It would mean a long process of education, but these people loved the Bible, and they persisted in asking her for more and more opportunities for Bible study.

Pastor Johnson's experience is not so different from others who have sought to focus on or develop a common vision of social ministry within a congregation. Many of us myopically think that this mandate for ministry beyond our walls is clear to all Christians. How disappointing to discover that is often not the case. Congregations seem given to a natural inwardness. When this tendency is left unchecked, the result is an assumption—often unarticulated—that the social service tasks in our society are not the business of the Christian community, at least not of this congregation. More often than not such attitudes surface when the biblical foundation of the mission of the church has been neglected. Then, narrow understandings of the congregation's purpose flourish.

This book will help develop a study such as the one Pastor Johnson is planning because it focuses on the mission of the church in social service as it arises from the pages of Scripture. An auditory metaphor may be helpful in describing my approach. A professor of homiletics is fond of saying that the preacher needs to listen to two worlds, as if she or he were listening to the two channels of stereophonic music. In one ear are the sounds produced by the biblical text; in the other are the sounds heard from the congregation. Good preaching requires that the two channels of the headset be kept in balance.

This same analogy applies to the study and task of social ministry. One ear of the church needs to be attentive to the biblical message; the other needs to be tuned into the contemporary society. Only when the volume and balance are adjusted equally is the church able to know what motivates and how it is to undertake its ministry.

The same balance needs to be achieved in biblical studies focusing on social ministry. My plan for such a study is to listen with equal attentiveness to both the biblical witness and the contemporary society and congregation. With our listening so balanced, the plan can be summarized in two basic biblical questions: Who is God? (what has God done and what will God continue to do?); and Who are we as the people of God (what has God made of us, asked of us, and promised us?) Answers to these two questions are sought in the two parts of this book. Part One sketches as concisely as possible the biblical reasons for social ministry. First, the biblical motivations for social ministry are rooted in the dominant images of God articulated in the Old

Testament (chap. 1). Second, the Jesus image of God is the decisive confirmation that for Christians God is one who cares about the total life conditions of all humans (chap. 2). Third, the community of God's people is commissioned as God's agents of care for persons (chap. 3). Finally, the images of the future promised by God suggest the direction and goals of our ministry in society, while motivating us to join forces with God to achieve these goals (chap. 4).

Part Two attends more to the other channel (our contemporary situation) without tuning out the first (the biblical witness) as it outlines two practical sets of tasks for social ministry as suggested by response to the basic questions (Who is God, and who are we as the people of God?). These two tasks need to be addressed by congregations as they are moved to enact their sense of social ministry. But in doing so, they are aided by the resources of the biblical witness. The first task is nurturing in the congregation and in society as a whole a mentality or consciousness for, or at least congenial to, social ministry (chap. 5). The second task is to address the realistic fears that become common barriers to social ministry (chap. 6). The conclusion finds the taproot of social ministry in the theology of the church's mission arising from the words of the risen Christ to his disciples.

PART ONE

Biblical Images for Social Ministry

1

Old Testament Images of God

Who we are gives expression to the God we worship. More than our recitation of creeds, the way we live and the opinions we express betray our concept of what we hold to be the ultimate reality. At a fundamental level the social ministry of the church arises from an image of God founded on the biblical witness. The basic question then becomes the image of God operative in a congregation. If the image is that of the biblical God, there is a resultant desire for a ministry to society. But people may have become hostages of a miniature, if not a false, deity. The most commanding force in our lives—shaping the way we live and the distribution of our energies—is our concept of God.

To address the biblical roots for social ministry means, therefore, to begin with the biblical images of God. For in those images the call to social service in the name of Christ is heard. It becomes necessary to attempt to understand the major motifs in the biblical portrayal of God, and that enterprise begins with the Hebraic images of God preserved for us in the Hebrew Scriptures that we Christians refer to as the Old Testament.

The phrase "images of God" is employed for a number of reasons. The word "image" is intended to suggest, first, that any portrayal of the ultimate reality, including the biblical ones, is at best a human perception of a reality that lies beyond the boundaries of language and conception. All the ways in which we speak of God represent efforts to understand the absolute unknowable in terms of the known. Therefore, the images of God in Scripture and theology are really metaphors in the sense that they attempt to speak of the divine reality as analogous to human realities.[1]

"Images" moreover implies that there is no single, logically consistent picture of the divine in the pages of Scripture, but rather a variety of portrayals, each of which captures some vital experience of God. This variety of images arises out of human contexts—historical circumstances, cultural patterns, and the human needs of the time. If we were left with only one such image, the claims that Scripture presents some sort of authoritative revelation of the divine in a variety of human contexts would be incredible. The fact that there are numerous such images allows us to find patterns and recurring themes, and precisely in those patterns and themes Christians claim revelation is encountered.

The thesis of this chapter and the next is that among that variety of images there is a remarkably consistent theme, namely, that the biblical God cares passionately about the total welfare of all humans. That theme will be distilled from within the major types of literature found in the Old Testament, and in conclusion a number of "counter-images" that confront us on the pages of the Hebrew Bible will be acknowledged.

The God of Creation

Genesis 1 and 2 present the image of the creator God, who forms reality through the power of the divine word (Genesis 1) or act (Genesis 2). Interest in these provocative chapters, however, is herein restricted to one dimension of that picture of God, namely, the divine origin of material reality.

The biblical creation stories depict God creating matter and then declaring it "good" (e.g., 1:25). Included in that material creation is the human being, created in the "image" of God. In the creation story in chapter 2 the material character of human life is more vividly portrayed than in the first. Adam is formed from the "dust of the ground" (v. 7) and Eve from the physical body of Adam (vs. 21-22). But in both stories it is clear that the material dimension of the human reality originates from the craft of God. That dimension is, then, the realization of the will of God. In opposition to any perspective that depreciates the material realm as evil or less than the will of God, these stories unequivocally affirm matter as having its existence in God.

Two things in particular are to be noted. First, the material realm is good and the result of the creative intent of God. Therefore, humans cannot minimize the importance of matter without doing violence to the biblical image of God as Creator.

Second, humans themselves are material creatures. It is not that the material dimension of human life is outside of the compass of the divine will, but rather is integral to it. The creation stories affirm that materiality is absolutely constitutive of what it means to be human. There is no concept of humanity here except that of a material humanity. Who I am is in large part comprised of my physical body— my materiality. Whatever may have been intended by the "image of God," it is clear from the text of Genesis 1:26-30 that it is humanity in its materiality, not apart from it, that is in the image of God. Nothing in the text suggests that God's "image" is a purely spiritual entity contained within an inferior physical body. Furthermore, human existence is part of a total material creation—an integral part of the whole of creation.

The creation stories honor and celebrate the physical realm as the result of a divine creative act. The implications are that humans must be understood as a delicate and inseparable whole in which matter is integral with the spiritual reality of life. Therefore, the corporeal character of humanity must be taken seriously.[2]

The image of God suggested by these stories is that of a Creator who intends the physical dimension of life for people. The material is not denigrated or subordinated to a higher dimension of the human whole. This view anticipates the way in which the biblical God is represented as one concerned for the full range of human life including the physical welfare of people. That fact becomes clearer with investigation of the other images of God in the Old Testament.

The God of the Exodus

Few contemporary scholars of the history of Israel would deny that the experience of the exodus from Egypt constitutes the formative experience for Israelite religion. Whatever historical truth resides behind the story of the patriarchs, the event of the release from bondage in Egypt supplied the raw historical data that was shaped into the crucial revelatory encounter of the people of Israel with their God.

That data, tradition would have us believe, was interpreted by the prophetic personages of Moses and Miriam. With the predominant image of God told in the exodus story, then, this survey continues. The story as it stands is a blending of different traditions that took literary form at different points in Israel's history but form a narrative whole. From that narrative drama of the exodus an image of God emerges that has a number of important features.

The Liberator

The Book of Exodus presents the struggle for the release of a group of slaves from Egyptian bondage as a dramatic combat between two divine claimants—Yahweh and Pharaoh. On one level, then, the success of the exodus was a victory for Yahweh over the Egyptian deities. On another level of more interest to us is the fact that the victory is a historical one (cf. Exod. 15:21).[3] The course of history is altered by virtue of the intervention of God through the prophetic agent Moses. That the definitive revelation of God for Israel is a historical one is important. It means that this God attends to the historical conditions of humans, that the historical realities of human existence are precisely where humans encounter God, and that history is therefore sanctioned as a "sacramental" access to God. That is to say, the material realm of time and space becomes the medium through which an encounter with God is experienced.

Israel understood the revelatory experience of the exodus as paradigmatic of the way in which God works in human life. The exodus is more than a past event, however crucial, in which God rescued a people from slavery. In biblical thought the exodus is the model for how God always and everywhere acts for human welfare. We need only remember the way in which the anonymous prophet of the exile, whom we call Deutero-Isaiah (Isaiah 40–55), understood the exodus to function as the pattern for God's new redemptive act in returning the people to their homeland (e.g., Isa. 43:16-17). We need only recall the way in which the Passover in celebration of the exodus became and remains the heart of Jewish piety. In the same pattern the early Christians interpreted the cross as a new Passover (e.g., 1 Cor. 5:7). Jews and Christians alike found in the exodus a way of understanding God and God's work among humans.

On what might appear to be a more mundane level, the exodus is presented as the story of the remarkable release of an oppressed minority from the abusive power of their oppressors. The primary revelatory event for the Old Testament is found in divine action that changed the social and economic conditions of a people. The struggle of that people was a class struggle between a minority group of immigrants and the oppressive practices of the established governmental powers. Like any oppressed people, the people of Israel in Egypt internalized their oppression, so that their spirits were broken under the weight of their oppression (Exod. 6:9). The exodus story portrays God as taking sides in that struggle, identifying with the oppressed against their oppressors, and aiding them in their resistance (e.g., Exod. 1:15-22).[4] The exodus God is depicted as one who is not bound by the human establishment but free to join in solidarity with the oppressed. What results is the liberation of a minority group. The liberation is from oppression and to a new future consisting of a homeland and an identity as the chosen people of God. Thus the exodus image is the image of a Liberator who acts in response to dreadful human conditions in an effort to alleviate those conditions.

Phrasing this theme differently will shed a different ray of light on it. Some Old Testament scholars and historians are arguing that Yahweh was known as "the God of the outsider" (the *ʿApiru*). The story of Israel is the tale of the emergence of a new people and nation forged from among those who stood outside of the common consensus of the established people of the time. The Hebrew slaves in Egypt were such outsiders—those who did not share in the Egyptian view of reality and justice. Those who were to align themselves with the former slaves when they made their entry into Canaan were also persons who had become alienated from the Canaanite way of life (cf. Joshua 24). Together these groups comprised the "underclass" of Egypt and Canaan, who by royal decree or by their own choice out of disillusionment with the system had become disenfranchised and estranged. Israel's origins, then, constituted a kind of rebellion on the part of such persons. Out of this motley assemblage of aliens, strangers to the established systems of governance, Yahweh created a new thing: a people of God. What forged their identity was the God who offered them an alternative to their enslavement and their isolation—the liberator God, Yahweh.[5]

The Passionate God

Undergirding the exodus story is the call of Moses. In the traditions concerning his call there is preserved a powerful image of this liberator

God. It is most clearly expressed in Exod. 3:7-12 (but cf. Exod. 6:2-8). There legend preserves how God confronts the exiled shepherd, Moses, with a commission. Moses is called to the task of being the human agent of God's liberation.

The words of God there are filled with language that attributes to God human perception and emotions. That attribution vividly betrays an important image of the divine. God says:

> I have observed the misery of my people . . . and have heard their cry . . . I know their sufferings, and I have come down to deliver them from the Egyptians, and to bring them out of that land to a good and broad land . . . the cry of the Israelites has now come to me; I have also seen how the Egyptians oppress them. So come, I will send you to Pharaoh to bring my people . . . out of Egypt. (3:7-10)

The verbs used of God are replete with a sensitivity to the conditions of the people: "observed," "heard," "know," and "come down to deliver." Consider the implications of such verbs. God is not unmoved by the plight of the people. On the contrary, the verbs suggest God's attentiveness to human welfare. Most important is that God is moved by the physical—the social, economic, political—conditions of the people.

The verb, "know," suggests even more. It is a form of the Hebrew verb, *yadah,* that means more than knowing in the sense of a cognitive perception, which would amount to little more than the verbs "see" and "hear." The Hebrew verb means to know in the sense of sharing in the reality of the known. So, the word could be used of the sharing of two human lives in sexual intercourse (e.g., Gen. 4:25). The import of the word here is the hint that God not only is sensitive to the suffering of the people but shares in their suffering.[6] In "knowing" the suffering of the people God is made to declare that the divine reality participates in their life conditions.

Several views are ruled out by the impact of this passage. Any sense that the biblical God is removed from passionate concern is eliminated. Any concept of a God who does not suffer is immediately contradicted. Nor is the God imaged for us in this passage a passive figure. Moved by the plight of the people, God declares the intention to act on behalf of the people—"I have come down to deliver." It is not enough that the people know there is a deity who is sensitive to their condition. That may be comforting in some ways, but it is not enough for this God. God is volitional and intentional—willing an action. The excuse is sometimes made, "I feel for you, but I can't reach you." This is not a God who feels for the hurt of the people who are out of the divine reach. The act to free Israel is designed with one purpose in mind, namely, to change the conditions of the people.

It should be said in passing that the mode of action is through human agency. Moses is sent in order to execute God's plan of action. How does the liberating, passionate God act? Through humans who are commissioned to represent the divine will. The magnitude of that feature notwithstanding (cf. chap. 3 below), suffice it for now to note the vital role to which the human, Moses, is assigned; humans are enlisted for the cause of their own liberation.

The Expense of Liberation

The image of the God of the exodus must be concluded with one further point. The act of liberation initiated by the compassion of God is an expensive one. Our modern sensitivities are offended by the infliction of suffering on the Egyptians, graphically narrated in the tradition of the plagues (Exodus 7–13). Why, we rightly ask, must the liberation of Israel bring such suffering for the Egyptians? If God sides with the oppressed against the oppressors, does that justify the visitation of such pain on the oppressors? Does the divine compassion not include those who are themselves victimized by their oppression of others?

The story of the plagues on the Egyptians has doubtless been shaped by the natural human feelings of revenge and anger. In the narrative of those terrifying events Israel found a catharsis for their anger toward their oppressors. Still, there is a truth preserved for us in that dimension of the exodus story. That truth is that liberation is always expensive. The liberation of the oppressed always costs someone something. In this case, the exodus story graphically portrays the fact that the liberation of an oppressed minority is accomplished only at the expense of the oppressors. The story of the plagues suggests the way in which the relief of human plight means that a basic societal change must be accomplished and that such change entails suffering. History witnesses to the truth of this insight again and again. The change that a society must experience to alter the conditions of an economically and socially oppressed group requires that some bear the suffering of that change. American society in the last quarter of the twentieth century has learned that the relief of the oppression of

racial minorities and women necessarily involves corrective measures
that result in painful transitions for the majority. For instance, "quotas"
in hiring minorities and women are in truth a kind of "reverse discrimination." More accurately, however, they are the injustices suffered by the oppressors in order that justice for the oppressed might
be realized. They are the expenses of liberation.

What, then, of the message that God takes sides with the suffering
people against those responsible for their suffering? Does such a view
minimize the breadth of the compassion of God? Perhaps God does
not reject one party by siding with the suffering party. God can feel
love for the oppressors, even while engaged in the task of breaking
their grasp on the oppressed. If parents witness their six-year-old
beating mercilessly on a three-year-old sibling, they intervene to re-
strain the older child. Yet such an action on behalf of the victim does
not mean the parents cease to love and care for the older child. In
fact, the parents' love for the older child cannot permit them to allow
her or him to continue to act in such a destructive manner. By freeing
the younger child they also rescue the elder from his or her behavior.
So, perhaps God's compassion for the oppressor is not reduced by the
necessity of intervening on behalf of the oppressed. Even given the
fact that liberation is going to cost the oppressor dearly, the exodus
God is still the loving creator of the oppressor as well as the oppressed.

The image of God in the exodus sets a pattern for the way God
is portrayed throughout the major streams of Old Testament tradition.
It is an image of a God whose concern is with the historical arena of
human existence; a God who acts to liberate humans from conditions
of suffering and deprivation; a God who is sensitive to and shares the
suffering of humans; and a God who shares in the reality of the cost
of liberation. The image of God in the covenant and the law of the
Old Testament is little different.

The God of the Covenant and the Law

The exodus cannot be isolated from the covenant and the law. In the
Old Testament the covenant arose as a result of the liberation of the
people from bondage in Egypt. In turn the law became a major component of the covenant. As these three are linked with each other in
a chain of cause and result, so the images of God in each of the three
components are remarkably consistent.

The covenant with the people of Israel was an agreement rooted in the exodus experience. The covenant statement found in Exod. 19:4-6 begins, "You have seen what I did to the Egyptians, and how I bore you on eagles' wings and brought you to myself" (cf. Deut. 5:6). The liberation from oppression is the premise on which the covenant agreement is based. But the covenant declaration continues with the consequence of that liberation: "Now therefore, if you obey my voice and keep my covenant, you shall be my treasured possession out of all the peoples." The exodus represents the initiative of God in establishing a relationship with the people. But from that initial act of God on behalf of the people surfaces their responsibility in the new relationship.

Out of the new covenantal relationship flows the demand for obedience. In the words of James Limburg, the pattern is that of "three R's": the "reminder" of the exodus is the basis of the "relationship" established in the covenant that calls for the "response" of the people in obedience.[7] Obedience is motivated by the response of gratitude for what God has done in the exodus and in creating the covenant relationship with the people. Human obedience is not the initial element but only the reaction to the outpouring of divine care and compassion.

With this understanding of the covenant relationship it is important to note several things about the character of the Old Testament legislative materials. First, it presupposes the relationship of the covenant. It is not designed to make the people of Israel acceptable to God. The action of God in freeing the people and relating to them through the covenant was already evidence of their acceptance in the mystery of divine election. The sole motive for keeping the law in the Old Testament was that of grateful acknowledgment of what God had already done for Israel.

Second, the law is the human side of the divine-human agreement. Obedience constitutes the obligation of the contractual agreement between Israel and Yahweh (e.g., Deut. 26:18). Therefore, obedience to the law is righteousness in the sense that it is remaining true to the relationship; it is faithfulness to that relationship.

Third, the law was intended to apply the relationship with God to every aspect of human life. In one sense it was the bridge between religion and everyday life. It overcame the gap between the sacred and the secular, between worship and life, between God and the mundane of daily existence. For that reason the law is filled with every kind of human experience and prescribes behavior for all realms of life (e.g., sex, diet, as well as worship). The Hebraic law is a remarkable and ambitious undertaking in that it casts the beam of religious faithfulness into every imaginable darkened corner of life for the people of the time.

(4)   Fourth, the law was an effort to fashion a culture for the people of Israel. In its primitive beginnings the law initiated a process of shaping the motley group of freed slaves into a society. The law prescribed what it meant to be Hebrew, an Israelite. It shaped the foundations of a culture that was distinguished by its moral character.

(5)   Finally, and most important, the law expresses the character of God. Because God is concerned with human conduct and character, humans must be concerned. The law is the supreme expression of what has been said to be the genius of Israelite religion—a moral theism. The law is law precisely because it is the expression of the divine will. There is no other rationale for the law in the Old Testament. The sabbath regulation is not justified on the basis of the humanistic need for a day of rest. The dietary laws are not supported on the basis of nutritional health. They are asserted simply as commands of God. The laws are windows into the Hebraic conceptions of God. They inform us of how the people of Israel came to conceive the nature of the God they worshiped. They offer us glimpses into the concern of God for the welfare of humans.

Amid the vast bodies of legislative material, we are interested in only a few samples of those laws that suggest the Hebraic image of God as one who cares for the needy and suffering human. Admittedly the picture is not a simple, consistent one, and we shall discuss one notable exception below. But the evidence is convincing enough to posit an image of God as the compassionate advocate of the poor, for the victim of misfortune, and for the mistreated.

Advocate of the Poor

There is a preponderance of legislation concerned to establish a means by which the hungry are fed. Two vivid examples are sufficient for our purposes. Leviticus 19:9-10 prescribes the practice of intentionally careless harvesting for the purpose of making food available to the needy. The reaper is to leave the borders of the field untouched; the grape pickers are not to strip the vines bare nor gather the grapes that have fallen to the ground: "You shall leave them for the poor and the alien."

Deuteronomy 23:24-25 goes a step farther. It sanctions the entering of another's field, to eat one's fill of the produce. It guards against the abuse of such privilege by limiting the quantity that can be taken, but it acknowledges the reality of the hungry and renders anyone's field a source of food.

What is instructive about these passages is that God is made to create a system whereby those who are plentiful supply the needs of those who want. It is a system of welfare in the best sense of the concept—a societal structure that enhances the welfare of those who have suffered misfortune.

Such a system is evident in a number of other passages concerned with the poor and indebted. Exodus 22:25 protects the Israelite from the deadly trap of indebtedness by denying a lender the right to collect interest on money borrowed. The next verse suggests that the indebted person has the right to the basic necessities of life. "Your neighbor's cloak," if taken as collateral for a loan, must be returned by sunset, because it may be the debtor's only protection against the cold of the night. By means of this legislation humans are never stripped of their basic right to shelter, no matter how great their debt may be. Basic human dignity must be honored, even in the case of the most destitute.

Thus an image is conjured of God as the advocate of the poor, the hungry, and the indebted. As the liberator God of the exodus sided with the oppressed against deliberate oppressors, the advocate God sides with those who may be oppressed by the circumstances of life. The God of the law stands in solidarity with the poor and insists on their rights and dignity. The legislation gives us a peek into the Israelite image of a caring God.

Another dimension of God's advocacy of the poor which emerges is that it is the responsibility of the wealthy to change the condition of the poor. It is the responsibility of the person with an ample farm to share the produce with the needy. Those who have resources are responsible to make loans and not to subject the debtor to unjust suffering. This is the reverse of an argument often heard among us that it is the responsibility of the poor to improve their lot. Bruce C. Birch has observed, "Thus, the responsibility for initiative lay with the privileged rather than with the dispossessed themselves, even as God had taken the initiative to deliver Israel."[8]

Advocate of Justice

The image of God as the advocate of the poor and needy is one part of the image of God as the advocate of justice in general. The justice of God for human welfare is evident in many ways in the Old Testament legal materials, but nowhere is it more radically portrayed than in the provision for the Sabbatical and Jubilee years.[9]

The Sabbatical and Jubilee years are related traditions in the Hebrew Scriptures. The Sabbath year legislation is found within the Covenant Code of Exodus 21–23 and the Deuteronomic Code (Deuteronomy 15). In the first God is pictured as the monarch of the people and as their social liberator. A number of provisions are legislated for the seventh year. Slaves are to be released along with their families (Exod. 21:2-6). The land is to be given a sabbatical rest by leaving the fields fallow. Any crops the land might spontaneously produce during the fallow year could be harvested by the stranger or the poor (Exod. 23:10-11).

In the Deuteronomic Code there is provision for the care of the poor (Deut. 15:1-18) that includes the cancellation of all debts (vs. 1-6), lending to the poor (vs. 7-11), and the freeing of Hebrew slaves (vs. 12-18). This legislation differs from that in Exodus in that slaves are to be released with provisions so that they may start a new life, and women are explicitly included. It is instructive that 15:15 roots the release of the slaves in Israel's own liberation from slavery in the exodus event.

The provisions for the Jubilee year (the fiftieth year) are found in Leviticus 25. They are premised on the belief that God is the royal owner of the land and the only one who can legislate its use and possession. The chapter is divided into six provisions: first, the calculating and proclaiming of the Jubilee is prescribed (vs. 8-10a); second, the return of real estate to its original owner or the family to which it was originally allotted is required (vs. 10b and 13); third, provision is made for the fallow year for the soil (vs. 11-12); fourth, the sale and redemption of real estate is demanded (vs. 14-17 and 23-28); fifth, special provision is made for the treatment of land in Levitical cities (vs. 29-34); finally, slaves are to be redeemed from their condition (vs. 39-43 and 47-55). Debts that necessitated the indenture of persons and/or families are apparently to be canceled. (The earliest form of slavery in Israel seems to have been a kind of welfare system in itself, for it allowed the possibility that if circumstances became so bad one could sell himself and his family into slavery. In that state the family would at least be privileged to the basic necessities of life.)

The Jubilee laws would have had sweeping social effects in at least three ways. They would have affected the entire nation and not

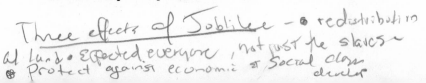

[Handwritten margin notes: God; Jubilee Laws; 1. Date 2. return of real estate 3. fallow year 4. Sale & redemption of Land 5. Land in Levitical 6. Redeem Slaves]

[Handwritten bottom notes: Three effects of Jubilee — redistribution; a) Land expected everyone, not just the slaves; b) Protect against economic & social class divider]

just certain contracts. They would have covered non-Israelites with Hebrew slaves. They would have brought about a radical redistribution of the land. Such redistribution would guard against the tendency for land to become increasingly the possession of a privileged few in the society and would protect against the emergence of social and economic classes. The provisions of the Jubilee year represent a means of drastically reordering a society. They provide a structure that abruptly reforms any injustice that has over time crept into the community.

There is serious debate about the Jubilee year: scholars are unsure whether or not it was ever observed. It certainly would have been resisted by the empowered, those who stood to lose a great deal if the Jubilee year were observed. Furthermore, whether it was intended as a single observance or one to be repeated every fiftieth year is not clear. Nevertheless, evidence of the tradition is found in several places in the Old Testament, for example, Isa. 61:1-2, Jer. 34:8-22, and Neh. 5:1-13.

What is of interest to us is the image of God portrayed in the Sabbatical and Jubilee provisions. It is the image of an advocate of social justice. God is pictured as the sovereign of the nation, enacting radical economic and social reform that restores justice where it has been obviated. God speaks in this legislation as one identified with the poor, the enslaved, and the dispossessed, as well as one who is concerned for the welfare of the natural environment. The divine voice of the legislator in this case, as in so many others throughout the Old Testament legal codes, is that of one who is committed to the promotion of the physical welfare of the people and the preservation of the physical environment. God speaks on behalf of those whose condition has deprived them of the power to speak forcefully and effectively for themselves.

The God of the covenant and the law is the advocate of those suffering poverty and injustice. The laws are the means by which Israel's God might rule in their midst. What does it mean for God to reign? For the God of the covenant and law to reign in the lives of the people meant above all that social justice be done, especially with regard to those whose condition had stripped them of power to effect change in their own lives.

The God of the Prophets

Moving out of the Torah into the prophetic literature of the Old Testament, we continue to encounter a God who again and again is the advocate of the poor and mistreated, the protector of social justice. The classical prophets, whose messages are represented for us in written form, concur in their insistence that God's rule of Israel encompasses the social life of the people. As spokespersons for that rule the prophets articulate four particular demands of God for a just society.

Just Social Relationships

First, many of the prophets speak of God's demand for just relationships within the society. There is a special emphasis on just relationships between the rich and the poor. Amos is vivid in his description of the contorted relationships of eighth-century Israel: "They sell the righteous for silver and the needy for a pair of sandals—they . . . trample the head of the poor into the dust of the earth" (2:6b-7a). The rich are said to "oppress the poor" and "crush the needy" (4:1). In the same century Micah attacks the unjust means by which the powerful scheme to acquire land at the expense of others (2:1-2). Jeremiah is just as stern in his depiction of the failure of Judah nearly two hundred years later. He speaks of the practice of the rich to catch persons, like trappers catch animals, in order that the rich might grow all the more richer (5:26-27).

The demand of the rule of God is for just relationships within the society. That justice must especially be practiced with regard to those most vulnerable to abuse—the poor and needy. Again, God is identified with those who are most likely to suffer in a society, especially one in which some are affluent.

Justice of Political Leaders

Israel's monarchy was founded on the assumption that the king was God's designated representative on earth (the "anointed"). The king is supposed to possess a special relationship with God (that is sometimes expressed in the title, "son of God," e.g., Ps. 2:7) and be capable of knowing and doing the divine will. Israel's monarchy was theoretically a kind of "constitutional monarchy" in which it was God who served as the sovereign of the land and even of the king. Therefore, the political leaders in particular were held responsible for enacting the will of God for the people.

The mistreatment of the poor is often laid at the feet of the rulers of the nation. Micah is most intense in his portrayal of the rulers.

> You who hate the good and love the evil,
> who tear the skin off my people,
>   and the flesh off their bones;
> who eat the flesh of my people
>   flay their skin off them,
> break their bones in pieces,
>   and chop them up like meat in a kettle,
>   like flesh in a caldron (3:2-4).

In the context of oracles against the king, Jeremiah speaks of the injustice of building one's house by unrighteousness, concluding, "But your eyes and heart are only on your dishonest gain, for shedding innocent blood, and for practicing oppression and violence" (22:13-17). The rulers of the people have a special responsibility before God in protecting the rights of the lowly against the empowered.

The rulers of the nation are entrusted with the obligation to enact the justice that is characteristic of God. Their betrayal of the trust is a serious offense. Moreover, this singling out of the rulers suggests the way in which those with power are tempted to use that power for their own ends, and most often at the expense of the powerless. In this regard, a story of one of the earlier prophets is germane. It is the tale of Nathan's confrontation of David after the king has successfully had Bathsheba's husband, Uriah, killed (2 Samuel 11 and 12). It is the voice of God through the prophet that cries out against the exploitation of the powerless by the empowered.

Social Morality with Worship

Surely one of the greatest contributions of the prophets is their insistence on the relationship of morality and worship. Religious ceremonies are pointless and dishonest without just and right dealings with others, Amos insisted (5:21-24). Micah's words on the subject are well known. In the context of a legal trial in which the people are accused by God of having broken the covenant, Micah sarcastically gives the people's defense: "With what shall I come before the Lord?" Does God expect burnt offerings, thousands of rams and rivers of oil, the offering of one's own children for the atonement of sin? The response of the prosecutor representing God is a classic: "He has told you . . . what is good; and what does the Lord require of you but to do justice, and to love kindness, and to walk humbly with your God? (6:6-8).

Micah 5

Jeremiah's attack on temple worship in his own day is equally pointed. The injustices of the worshipers have made the temple into a "den of robbers," for they have failed to "act justly one with another" and instead "oppress the alien, the orphan, and the widow." They steal and murder, yet come into the place of worship and declare, "We are safe!" (7:5-11). Jeremiah goes on to claim that God never desired burnt offerings and sacrifices, but only obedience (7:21-23).

A faithful relationship with God demands just relationships with other people far more than it requires proper worship. The character of God revealed in the covenant and the law makes clear that the worship of this God is by means of moral and righteous behavior as well as sacrifice and praise. The pigeon-holing of worship and daily life is impossible, since God is a moral God, concerned above all else with the relationships among persons.

Inclusiveness

The prophets sound the demand for inclusiveness in their concern for other people. The struggle in the history of Israel between an exclusion of those who were not Israelite and an inclusion of such persons is a long and complicated one. But the prophets broadcast the demand of God for the people to open their lives to the needs of all humans. Deutero-Isaiah conceived of Israel as the means by which God brought justice upon the entire world (Isa. 42:5-9). The successor of Deutero-Isaiah in the Isaianic tradition announced God's intent that the new temple be "a house of prayer for all peoples" (56:7).

Amid voices of exclusion and separateness, an unknown prophet composed the short story we know as the Book of Jonah. It is a poignant and humorous tale of a bigoted, self-righteous prophet, who refuses to proclaim the mercy of God for inhabitants of Nineveh, the capital city of the hated enemy, the Assyrians. The prophet's words of lament after the residents of that city had repented summarize the message of the book: "I knew that you are a gracious God and merciful, slow to anger, and abounding in steadfast love"—for, we might add, even the Assyrians (Jon. 4:2).

While the struggle for such an image of God as one whose love was inclusive of the foreigner and even the enemy is never finally resolved in the pages of the Old Testament, the prophetic voices can be heard there, calling for a comprehension of inclusive divine care. The importance of these voices to this study is that they suggest that

God's concern for human welfare is not limited to those of a particular religious community.

Summary

[handwritten annotation: Prophet's themes: ① Just treatment of needy ② Good leadership of nation ③ interrelatedness of Worship & Social Morality ④ inclusiveness of God's Care]

Demands for just treatment of the needy, the obligations of the leaders of the nation for justice, the interrelatedness of worship and social morality, and the inclusiveness of God's care for humans are among the prominent themes of the prophets. They offer us an image of a God whose rule extends to the social realm. So important is this social rule of God that the prophets are forthright in declaring that the violation of that rule can only result in the punishment of the people. Hence, the prophets of the eighth and sixth centuries understood that the exiles of both the northern kingdom of Israel and the southern kingdom of Judah are the direct consequences of social injustice (e.g., Amos 3:1-2). The violation of God's will for social relationships is a matter of utmost significance. Its punishment arises from the very nature of God, for whom societal structures are of paramount concern.

The God of the Psalmists

The social concern of the God of the Hebrew Scriptures is also expressed in the Psalms, which are instructive especially because it is in worship that a people give clearest expression to their image of God. How worship is done always tells us something vital about people's understanding of the one to whom worship is addressed. The Psalms represent the corpus of the literature of Israelite worship and hence bear attention. Within the vast variety of themes and moods depicted in the Psalms there is an amazing consistency in the portrayal of God, which in turn fits the pattern of the images we have examined.

The God addressed in the Psalms is frequently represented as an advocate for and a rescuer of the poor. God raises up the needy (107:41) and is the savior of the poor (34:6). The afflicted are defended by God (140:12). God is present with the needy (109:31) and reverses the human conditions of want and deprivation (113:5-9), rescuing the needy (146:5-9).

The God of the Psalms is also the liberator of the oppressed. God will see justice done (10:17) and respond to those in bondage (69:32-33).

[handwritten annotation in right margin: Savior of the poor God]

Moreover, God is the source of justice for the rulers and for the nations. It is from God that the king is given a just and righteous reign (72:1-4, 12-14). God is the hope of a nation for justice (82:3-4)and the hope of the needy and poor of the nation (10:18). It is God who will provide for just judgment (98:9), for God is just (99:4).

The psalmists who address God in these hymns repeatedly portray themselves as poor (e.g., 9:9-10; 86:1-2, 7). The Psalms are the petitions of the afflicted (25:16), the needy (35:10), the lowly (147:6), the downtrodden (74: 21), the orphans and widows (68:6), the children (116:6), and the barren woman (113:9). The impression one gains from this overview of the self-identification of the Psalmists is that God is one who hears the cries of the needy and oppressed. Indeed, it is the God of the exodus, who declares, "I have observed the misery of my people . . . and have heard their cry . . . I know their sufferings, and I have come down to deliver them . . ." (Exod. 3:7-8).

With the Psalms we have come full circle in the images of God and back to the primary image of the liberator of the oppressed. The literature of Israelite worship shows the influence of the Hebraic tradition that we have seen in the creation and exodus stories and in the legal and prophetic literature.

Counter-images

The diversity of the views in the Old Testament makes it inevitable that there not be unanimity on the images of God in that literature. The Hebrew Scriptures arose from the people over the course of at least nine centuries. They are folk literature in the sense that they give expression to the spirit of the common people. Within the unity of the views isolated here, diversity is unavoidable. It is important for us to note here a number of counter-images in that diversity, counter-images that represent a different view of God in relationship to human need and suffering. The human spirit is divided in its attitude toward the physical needs of others, and these counter-images represent the reservations humans often feel when confronted with those who suffer want and need.

Exclusion of the Afflicted

The Holiness Code of Leviticus 17–26 presents one of the counter-images. It is grounded in the understanding of the holiness of God

that requires a holiness of those who would worship this God (Lev.
11:44). The principle is the same as what we have seen in the legal
and prophetic literature: Because God is moral, the people of God
are required to live morally. In this case, the holiness of God dictates
a holiness about Israel. In the effort to discern what it meant to be a
holy people, Israel tried to define in its body of legislation appropriate
activity and character. What might it mean to be holy as God is holy
(Lev. 11:45)?

The priests who served before God in the temple were to be free
of anything that might compromise their worthiness. Among the
requirements, therefore, were moral character and bodily wholeness.
No one with a "blemish," namely, blindness, lameness, bodily mal-
formation, injury, or disease, could present an offering to God. A
person afflicted with any of these "blemishes" could participate in
worship but not serve as a priest (Lev. 21:16-23).

[margin handwriting: no bodily blemees]

Closely associated with holiness is the concept of ritual cleanness.
A system of taboos originated out of a basic concern for self-preservation that took on religious importance. Uncleanness, it was believed,
was communicated by touch or even association with that which was
considered unclean (Lev. 5:3). Certain human conditions came to be
regarded as endangering cleanness. In particular it was believed that
leprosy was a form of uncleanness and contact with the leper en-
dangered one's religious condition (Num. 5:2-4). Discharges from the
body were likewise regarded as defiling of cleanness. Menstrual blood
was thought to be unclean (Lev. 15:19), as was persistent discharge
of blood (Lev. 15:25), emission of semen (Lev. 15:16), and the discharge associated with childbirth (Lev. 12:2-5).

[margin handwriting: unclean]

The implications of these views for the ill and afflicted had unfortunate effects. Since holiness involved bodily wholeness and health,
it implied that anyone with a physical "blemish" was excluded from
holiness. Leprosy and any disease that involved bodily discharges
brought the status of "unclean."

[margin handwriting: no discharges]

The implied image of God in this legislation is that of one who
holds in low regard those with certain afflictions. Such persons are
excluded from the priestly functions and viewed as unclean before
God. While the hygienic reasons for such views are, in some cases,
understandable, it is tragic that the views were given religious sanction. The classification of bodily afflictions as unholy and unclean
meant that God did not and could not favor them. This image of God
had the result of creating a class of persons whose physical conditions
excluded them from the possibilities of religious favor. An image of

God sanctioned the formation of a class of the excluded, the outcast.
Surprisingly, in the same bodies of legal materials in the Old Testament
we find both the images of God as advocate for the afflicted and as
disdainer of the afflicted.

Two ways or images of how God viewed his people

Exclusion of the Foreigner

Just as some of the legislation promoted the exclusion of the physically
afflicted, so are the non-Israelites sometimes excluded from the realm
of God's concern. In the Old Testament God occasionally appears to
care about the welfare of the people of Israel, but to have no concern
for others. This view of God constitutes another counter-image to the
pattern we have discerned above.

For instance, in some cases the laws that protected the rights of
the poor and needy pertained only to Israel and excluded all others.
A case in point is the legislation that prohibited usury as a means of
protecting those forced to borrow money. That protection is explicitly
not extended to the non-Israelite (e.g., Deut. 15:3). The Sabbatical
release of the slaves in Exodus 21 specifically applies only to Hebrew
slaves (v. 2). In many cases, then, the image of the liberator God is
qualified by what appears to be the exclusion of the foreigner from
divine care.

As acknowledged above, the Old Testament demonstrates a long
struggle between two opposing tendencies in Israel's religious faith.
One was toward an exclusivism that stressed Israel's peculiar relationship with God and their privileged status as a chosen people of
God. The other was an inclusivism that arose from their emerging
monotheism and in turn led them toward an acknowledgment of the
worth of all people. We have already witnessed the inclusivistic thrust
of some of the prophets. Whenever Israel's own existence as a nation
and culture was threatened, the exclusivistic impulse tended to dominate. For now it is enough for us to recognize the way in which that
exclusivism was understood to be rooted in God. It is not that image
of God which wins the day—that is most dominant—but it is clearly
a reality in the Old Testament literature.

Divine Retribution

punish c illness & poverty
reward c health & material goods

A final counter-image to consider is that of God as one who punishes
wickedness with illness and poverty while rewarding righteousness

with health and material riches. Such an image of God is rooted in several Hebraic themes. The first is the belief sometimes witnessed in the literature of the Old Testament to the effect that the sovereignty of God means that all human conditions are due to the action of God. That view is summarized in the song of Hannah: "The Lord kills and brings to life; he brings down to Sheol and raises up. The Lord makes poor and makes rich; he brings low, he also exalts" (1 Sam. 2:6-7).[10]

Closely related and arising from that view is another. It is an ethical theory that God punishes and rewards through bringing certain life conditions. Such an ethical proposal is found running through the Old Testament like a continuous thread. It is found, for instance, at the heart of the view of history propagated by the school of Hebraic historians known as the deuteronomists. Judges 2:11-23 is a brief summary of the history of the Israelites in Canaan. It proposes that whenever Israel did evil it provoked God's anger and brought divine punishment in the form of defeats at the hand of their enemies. But hearing their cries of suffering, God would raise up among them a judge who would restore their fortunes. As soon as the judge died, the people would turn to evil again and the cycle would continue. The prophets clearly endorse the idea that national calamity was often the result of the intervention of God in judgment of the people.

On a personal level the so-called retribution ethic was a means of understanding the advent of misfortune as well as a way of explaining good fortune. For instance, leprosy is God's punishment of Miriam's disloyalty to Moses (Num. 12:9-10). David's faithfulness to God is the supposed reason for his success (1 Sam. 18:14). The violators of the law are threatened with poverty (e.g., Deut. 28:15-24 and Lev. 26:14-26), and riches are said to be a blessing bestowed by God for faithfulness (e.g., Job 42:10).

By the time of the return from exile the retribution ethic had become hardened into a dogma by which it was claimed the condition of a person was an index to her or his degree of religious faithfulness. Prov. 3:33-35 expresses the principle:

> The Lord's curse is on the house of the wicked,
>   but he blesses the abode of the righteous.
> Toward the scorners he is scornful,
>   but to the humble he shows favor.
> The wise will inherit honor,
>   but stubborn fools, disgrace.

That view is perhaps the root of a disdainful attitude toward the poor in certain of the Proverbs. The poor are lazy (6:6-11) and immoral (21:17; 23:21). Hence, suffering was understood as evidence of one's sinfulness, and freedom from suffering a sign of one's righteousness (e.g., Prov. 6:12-15). The so-called friends of Job each advocate this view (e.g., Job 4:7-9; 15:20; 36:14-16). They are dogmatic in their insistence that Job's plight must be an indication of his sinfulness and exhort him to confess to that sin.

What had occurred was the "reversal" of the logic that God punished and blessed with physical conditions. Now the condition of a person was the way by which one could know their sinfulness or righteousness and even the degree of one or the other. In spite of the challenge to this view mounted by the Books of Job and, in a less effective way, Ecclesiastes, this dogma persisted in Judaism into the time of Jesus as is evident from the New Testament (e.g., Luke 13:1-5 and John 9:1-4). That such a view is alive and well among us today is witnessed in the simple question that we so often ask of ourselves: "What have I done to deserve this?"

The image of God implicit in the retribution ethic especially in its later form stands in contradiction to the images of the God who cares about and sides with the suffering. It tends to make every victim in this world a sinner and to view anyone subjected to misfortune as the recipient of God's punishment. It is a conception of God which centers in the belief that God has rewarded the affluent and healthy while punishing the poor and afflicted.

Conclusion

Notwithstanding the counter-images, there resides in the Old Testament a recurring picture of God as one who suffers with the pain of humanity. That God is creator of the material dimension of human life, liberator of the oppressed, compassionate actor on behalf of the suffering, advocate of the poor and for justice, and a sovereign who demands just social relationships in addition to worship and requires an inclusive concern for others. The major stream of Old Testament thought is found in the cluster of these images of the God of social justice. The image with which the reader is persistently presented is that of a God who cares passionately about total human welfare.

It is on the foundation of those images that the social ministry of the church is built. That ministry takes as its goal the human enactment of the care and concern of the biblical God suggested by the major images of the Hebrew Scriptures. As our God identifies with the suffering and acts both to relieve and prevent suffering due to hardship and injustice, so Christians experience a solidarity with the poor, the afflicted, the oppressed, and the victimized. Because God has acted on behalf of such persons, so Christians act both to relieve and to prevent such suffering. It is our image of God above all else that makes us social ministers.

However, the counter-images suggest that God holds another view of the poor and suffering, and they comprise a different tributary in the Old Testament tradition which cannot be ignored. But the Christian looks beyond the Old Testament itself for some means of discerning which of these clusters of images represents the true God and which the distortions of the human mind and spirit. That confirmation is found in the images of God attributed to Jesus of Nazareth.

Notes

1. Cf. McFague, *Metaphorical Theology.*
2. This discussion is indebted to the essay by Sölle, "Between Matter and Spirit," 86–103.
3. Robinson, *Inspiration and Revelation*, Part 3.
4. Brown, *Unexpected News*, 33–48.
5. This suggestion arises from the work of Gottwald, *The Tribes of Yahweh* and *The Hebrew Bible*, as well as that of Walsh, *The Mighty from Their Thrones.* However, it is not necessary to agree entirely with their view of Israel's historical origins to be persuaded by the image of Yahweh as the God of the ᶜ*Apiru.*
6. On the theme of the suffering of God, cf. Fretheim, *The Suffering of God.*
7. Limburg, *The Prophets and the Powerless*, 26.
8. Birch, *The Old Testament Call*, 58.
9. For this discussion I thank Ringe, *Jesus, Liberation*, 16-32. Cf. Yoder, *The Politics of Jesus*, 64–77.
10. Cf. Ringgren, *Israelite Religion*, 47, 72–73.

2

The Jesus
Image of God

God is decisively revealed in the person and work of Jesus of Nazareth. That bold assertion stands at the heart of the Christian faith and comprises the major affirmation we make about God. All images of God are judged by a single norm—the God we believe we find manifested in the One who for us is the Christ. Just as a yardstick is used to determine the length of an object, Christ is our canon for measuring the truth of an assertion about the ultimate reality. God is made known to us in what Jesus believed about God, how Jesus spoke and acted, and supremely in Jesus' death and resurrection (John 1:18). Among other things Easter is God's affirmation of Jesus and his claims to know and reveal the divine identity. To inquire about the God revealed in Jesus is to ask a number of questions: What did Jesus expressly teach about God? What were his vital concerns? For his concerns inform us of God's concerns. What was the nature and form of his ministry? For that ministry expresses the mission of God in the world.

In the Jesus image of God, therefore, we seek affirmation of what we have claimed to be the major stream of the Old Testament images of God, namely, those that depict God as one concerned for the whole of human welfare. This chapter needs to address the question of the image of God implied in the Jesus story as reported to us in the Gospels. How is that image related to the picture of the liberator, the

31

passionate, active God who in the Old Testament exercises and demands social justice?

The following discussion bypasses the delicate question of the relationship of the historical Jesus to the portrayal of that figure in the four canonical Gospels. This is done on the basis of an important presupposition: The New Testament Christians accurately grasped and articulated the meaning of the ministry of the historical figure behind the Gospels. This is not to say that the Gospels are historically accurate in every case, but that the faith they express is a valid inference to be drawn from the historical facts.

Our discussion will center on three aspects of the Jesus image of God: the God who cares for the whole person, who cares for all persons, and who identifies with suffering humanity. These are obviously selected for the sake of the central concern of the book; other images, which are essential to any complete discussion of the Jesus image of God, are omitted.

The God Who Cares for the Whole Person

Remarkably, the ministry of Jesus, seen in its totality, expressed a concern for the whole of human existence. Every dimension of human life was addressed by either Jesus' actions or his words. It is important for our purposes to gain a bird's-eye view of that ministry to the whole person.

Physical Welfare

That Jesus addressed himself to the physical needs of humans is perhaps so obvious as to be trite. The healing stories, which make this immediately evident, dominate the Gospels both in their number and in their strategic locations. The Gospel of Mark, for instance, introduces the ministry of Jesus with the calling of the disciples (1:16-20) followed by a series of six references to healings in the course of thirty-six verses (1:21—2:12). In all four Gospels, the physical afflictions with which Jesus is concerned range from a simple fever (Mark 1:30-31) to the raising of the dead (John 11), suggesting that there is no physical affliction that did not evoke the attention of this Galilean itinerant.

But more than illness and affliction drew the attention of Jesus. The stories of the feeding of the multitudes found in all four of our

Gospels suggest a concern for the basic human condition of hunger (Matt. 14:13-21; 15:32-37; Mark 6:30-44; 8:1-10; Luke 9:10-17; John 6:1-13). Although these stories have meaning beyond satiating hunger, this primary level of meaning should not be lost to us. Surely they look forward to the way in which the ministry of Jesus anticipates the messianic banquet. They also have implications for the Sacrament of Holy Communion. But just as surely they demonstrate Jesus' care that a basic human need not go unfulfilled.

The dominance of the healing and feeding stories evidences the fact that the physical needs of humans are presented at the heart of Jesus' ministry. In Luke this presentation is made explicit with great clarity. Two passages figure prominently. Luke 4:16-21 narrates Jesus' appearance in the synagogue worship at Nazareth, where Jesus reportedly read from Isa. 61:1-2 (and 58:6).

> The Spirit of the Lord is upon me,
> because he has anointed me to bring good news to the
>   poor.
> He has sent me to proclaim release to the captives
> and recovering of sight to the blind,
> to let the oppressed go free,   *Case #3 - Ethics*
> to proclaim the year of the Lord's favor.

Upon completing the reading, Jesus boldly announced, "Today this scripture has been fulfilled in your hearing."

Luke depicts Jesus as understanding his ministry to be the fulfillment of God's concern to alter the physical conditions of the people of Israel. The hopelessness of those entrapped in poverty is lifted; the oppression of those in slavery is alleviated; and the affliction of blindness is overcome. It is possible that the "acceptable year of the Lord" is none other than the Jubilee year with its radical social reformation. To spiritualize this passage is to misunderstand the point Luke wants to communicate, as the second passage makes clear.[1]

In Luke 7:18-23 the third evangelist narrates a story of how the imprisoned John the Baptist sent messengers to Jesus with the crucial question, "Are you the one who is to come [i.e., the Messiah], or are we to wait for another?" Jesus' response is revealing. "Go and tell John what you have seen and heard: the blind receive their sight, the lame walk, the lepers are cleansed, the deaf hear, the dead are raised, the poor have good news brought to them. And blessed is anyone who takes no offense at me." Enlightening, is it not, that as

evidence he is indeed the long-awaited Messiah Jesus points to changes in the physical (and emotional) conditions of people as a result of
his ministry? Popular Christian mentality today might be inclined to
respond to John's question by pointing to the spiritual impact of Jesus'
ministry: souls are saved, the assurance of a life after death is bestowed,
peace of mind is given. Instead, Jesus lifts up the way in which his
ministry is yielding physical help for those whose lives have been
distorted by physical and social afflictions.

The tendency for contemporary Christians to spiritualize these
passages from the Gospel of Luke is deadly, especially when we are
seeking to nurture the biblical basis of social ministry. Why is it that
some are so inclined to read references to physical transformation in
spiritual terms? That is, why should anyone want to interpret blindness, lameness, leprosy, death, and poverty as symbols for ailments
in our internal lives having to do with our personal relationship with
God? One aspect is this: The New Testament lies in the hands of those
who are not afflicted with such physical ailments as these two Lukan
passages address. In an attempt to make Scripture relevant to the
situation of the well, free, and affluent, interpreters have understood
references to these physical and social conditions in a spiritual way.
The physical dimension of the human conditions transformed in the
ministry of Jesus is made into a mere vehicle of that gift of the Christ
event relevant to other needs, namely, spiritual matters. In that re-
grettable process another important relevance is lost—the call to continue the ministry of Jesus to those who suffer physical affliction
through what we term social ministry.

This propensity to spiritualize the ministry of Jesus to physical
needs is evident too in the way in which the Beatitude concerning
the poor is understood. That Beatitude is found in two forms in the
Gospels. The first is in Luke 6:20: "Blessed are you who are poor, for
yours is the kingdom of God." The second is in Matt. 5:3: "Blessed
are the poor in spirit, for theirs is the kingdom of heaven." It is
instructive that the second form of that Beatitude is by far the more
popular and is the one most readily quoted today. The danger of
spiritualizing the New Testament witness blinds us to even the most
obvious allusion to financial poverty.

The complex question of the tradition behind these two forms
of the Beatitude regarding the poor need not detain us here. But the
difference may not be as great as is so often thought. The Matthean
form may address the physically poor, just as does the Lukan form.

The poor became the model of piety for Judaism in that they acknowledged their own powerlessness and total reliance on God. Hence, the pious Jew might identify her or himself with the financially poor, so as to imitate their total dependence on God. The Matthean form of the Beatitude, therefore, may simply be an expansion that includes those who identify with the financially poor as well as the impoverished themselves.[2]

A further point is necessary. One of the counter-images of God present in the Old Testament is the understanding of affliction and illness as evidence of human sin and the divine punishment of that sin. In two different scenes in the Gospel narratives that perspective is expressed in questions posed to Jesus. In one case (Luke 13:1-5), Jesus is asked if he thought the sin of a number of Galileans who were martyred by Pilate was greater than the sin of other Galileans. His answer is an unequivocal no! He proceeds to cite another tragedy that had been given a similar interpretation and rejects any such reading of the tragedy. He then attacks the self-righteousness of the interrogators and warns them to repent. In another case (John 9:1-4), Jesus is asked if the affliction of a blind man was the result of that man's own sin or the sins of his parents. Jesus' answer in this case is very different. Neither sin occasioned the blindness of the man, but "that God's works might be revealed in him." He thereby decisively breaks the connection between sin and suffering. Then he points the disciples to their mission with him: "We must work the works of him who sent me." Jesus goes on to heal the blind man, and the man becomes a powerful witness to his healer.

The point is that Jesus absolutely rejected the notion that those who suffered physical illness or tragedy did so as a result of God's punishment of sin. He contradicted one of the images of God in the Old Testament that implies the absence of care for the afflicted and would tolerate none of its implications. Instead, he treated such persons with compassion and ministered to their need.

The picture is clear in both its bold lines and subtle shadings. Jesus reveals a God centrally concerned with the physical conditions of humans and acting through the Messiah to reverse bodily afflictions.

Emotional Welfare

The care of God for the emotionally afflicted is similarly represented in the ministry of Jesus, if in a somewhat more obscured way. The acts of forgiveness, of which there are several examples in the Gospels, express this theme (e.g., Luke 7:36-50). Forgiveness of sin addresses the emotional affliction of guilt and all that results from such an affliction.

But in the act of his exorcisms (the casting out of demons) Jesus is represented as healing what we today would understand as emotional illness. My intent is not to rationalize the exorcisms and reduce them to a form of psychotherapy. I propose, however, that demon possession was, in many but not all cases, the means by which the first-century Jewish world understood what the modern age has come to call neurosis and psychosis. In obvious ways the affliction of demon possession parallels serious emotional illness. It could result in self-infliction of wounds (e.g., Mark 5:5), the loss of basic skills, particularly speech and hearing (Matt. 12:22), seizures and convulsions (Luke 4:35; 9:42), and multiple personalities (Mark 5:9). Like emotional illness, demon possession produced pain and suffering, resulted in loss of the capacity for self-determination due to a power that seemed exterior to the individual, and manifested itself in a variety of socially undesirable behavioral and physical characteristics.

In his exorcisms Jesus expresses the concern of God for what we today term emotional health. Those acts of exorcism pervade the stories of Jesus in the first three Gospels. They are not peripheral but central to the picture of the ministry of Jesus those Gospels present. When we ignore the exorcisms, we ignore a sizable portion of the Gospel representation of Jesus' ministry. Moreover, we thereby ignore a crucial mandate for our own ministries. The exorcisms may be an embarrassing and strange phenomenon in the ministry of Jesus, but they embody a vital concern of God. The Jesus image of God is of one who cares not just for the physical but for the emotional well-being of humans as well.

The message of the exorcisms can be seen in another more general way. Albert Nolan has pointed out that the life of the common people of Jesus' day was filled with frustration, guilt, and anxiety. They were looked on as lawless and immoral because they were not educated in the Torah and because their circumstance in life did not allow them to engage in the study and meticulous application of the law of God as it was interpreted in that day. John 7:49 expresses this view of the common people. The Pharisees reportedly say of the people who followed Jesus, "This crowd, which does not know the law—they are accursed."

The consequent of being regarded with such aversion and even hostility took its toll in the spirit of the common people, Nolan contends. There was no way out of their predicament as sinners. They had to become reconciled to their destiny—their lot in life. Consequently, there was "a neurotic or near-neurotic guilt complex that led inevitably to fear and anxiety about the many kinds of divine punishment that might befall them." Out of this self-image, imposed on them by their religious leaders, there arose a propensity to mental illness that still further disabled the common people and made them dysfunctional.[3]

To just such people Jesus offered the message of the kingdom of God. It meant for them healing, forgiveness, acceptance, and hope for their lives. Jesus' ministry was directed toward just such pitiful and helpless people whose emotional conditions and societal standards entrapped them.

Economic Welfare

Something has been said already to suggest that the ministry of Jesus addressed itself to the economic welfare of humans. With his attention to the poor, Jesus expressed the care of God for the afflictions that come with impoverishment. But the point must be expanded here in several dimensions.

The first fact to be noted is that Jesus' ministry was spent to a large degree among the poor. This is clear from the convergence of three pieces of data. Jesus is represented as spending a good deal of his time among the common people of Palestine (e.g., see references to the "crowds" such as in Luke 6:17) and there were vast numbers of poor among the residents of that land in the first century of the Christian era. The Roman occupation had resulted in the dispossession of numerous farmers, and Herod the Great had furthered that process during his reign. As a result, there was more and more land in the hands of fewer and fewer, many of whom were foreigners and absentee landlords (e.g., the parable of the tenants, Matt. 21:33-46; Mark 12:1-12; Luke 20:9-18). Crop failures had only made the situation worse for the poor, many of whom were tenant farmers. Enormous taxation worsened the situation of the common people of the time. The taxes were of several kinds: The temple/priestly tax, the Roman tax (on property, per capita, custom taxes and tolls), the Herodian taxation, and the high interest on loans.[4]

But another bit of evidence points to the fact that much of Jesus' ministry was spent with the poor, namely, the way in which Jesus spoke of the poverty of his time. This is suggested in the parables, for instance. Jesus' story parables are noted for the manner in which they draw believable and realistic pictures from the common life of his hearers. Those parables offer us evidence of the poverty of his audience. The parable of the tenants (Matt. 21:33-43 and parallels) assumes the common knowledge of the number of farmers forced to work land that no longer belonged to them. The vineyard laborers (Matt. 20:1-15) takes for granted the enormous number of unemployed of the time. The lost coin (Luke 15:8-9) suggests the poverty of a household in which a single coin is precious. The figure of the poor man, Lazarus (Luke 16:19-31), implies the common sight of such a pitiful creature.

All of this indicates the way in which Jesus addressed himself to the poor of his time. But his other teachings also frequently deal with poverty and wealth. Suffice it to say that Luke represents Jesus as focusing extensive attention on the question of the dangers of wealth (e.g., 12:13-21), the proper use of riches (e.g., 19:1-10), and the call to surrender possessions for the kingdom of God (e.g., 18:18-23).[5]

But Jesus did more than speak about the need to respond to the condition of the poor and share possessions. His work took the form of a ministry for the poor by the poor. There is considerable debate over the issue of whether or not Jesus' own background was poverty, but a persuasive argument can be made that that was the case.[6] Regardless of the conclusion of that argument, there can be no argument about the fact that Jesus and his band of followers lived lives of poverty during the years of ministry. They constituted a group of itinerants dependent upon others for shelter and sustenance (e.g., Luke 8:1-3) and knew the experience of hunger (Mark 2:23-28). As Walter Pilgrim summarizes:

> What is important for us to see is that Jesus and his disciples belonged to those groups in society which did not produce their own economic sustenance, but rather by their unique service lived from the respect and gratitude and charity of others. This placed them socially and economically in the lower strata of society in the public years and doubtless brought them into close identification with the conditions and life-style of the poor. In this respect they were essentially one with them.[7]

In other words, Jesus shared a solidarity with the poor of his time.

Furthermore, the message of Jesus had a particular relevance to the poor. The advent of the kingdom of God meant the transformation of the economic conditions of the nation and the poor in particular. It implied a time of prosperity and plenty and the alleviation of poverty. The reign of God in the world was believed to bring a radical reordering of society, possibly represented in Jesus' saying, "So the last will be first and the first last" (Matt. 20:16; cf. 19:30; Mark 10:31; and Luke 13:30). The word of hope to the poor was that their condition would soon be transformed. Jesus' basic message, then, had a socially revolutionary quality that was directly relevant to those suffering impoverishment. This is the "good news" the poor hear preached to them (Luke 7:22) in the ministry of Jesus.

It is possible, too, that the so-called cleansing of the temple (Mark 11:15-17; Matt. 21:12-13; Luke 19:45-48; John 2:13-17) originally represented a social protest against the abuse of the poor by the wealthy of the religious establishment. The establishment was centered in the temple which had become its "den of robbers." Jesus' purpose in this dramatic act seems to have had little to do with a denouncement of the ritual worship performed in the temple, for the driving out of the money changers was done in the courtyard of the temple. There the traders and the money changers extracted outrageous sums from the common people who came to the temple to perform their religious obligations. Exorbitant prices were charged for the sacrificial animals. The money changers imposed a painfully heavy service charge for exchanging the currencies of the pilgrims to Jerusalem. What impressed Jesus was not the grandeur of the temple building but the offering of the widow (e.g., Mark 12:41-44). His act of driving the business people out of the courtyard was an act of protest against the economic exploitation that they brought to the religious life of Judaism.[8]

The image of God expressed in the ministry of Jesus is of one who cares about the economic condition of depravity. What we see and hear in Jesus are the outpourings of a heart that feels the pain of entrapment in poverty.

Social Welfare

It is a short step in our journey to reach another vantage point. From there we glimpse a view of Jesus' ministry as an articulation of God's concern for the social plight of persons. That has already been announced in Luke 4:16-21—the captives are released and the oppressed set free. The point must anticipate, too, some of what more properly belongs in the second major aspect of the Jesus image of God, namely, God's care for all persons. Still, the social welfare of people merits some observations in its own right.

First, Jesus' healings and exorcisms effected social integration as well as individual wholeness. Illness and affliction resulted in a process today known as "social marginalization." That is, physically afflicted persons were treated and regarded in such a way as to remove them from the mainstream of society. This was due in large part to the views of illness arising from the legislation regarding holiness and uncleanness discussed in chapter one.

A few examples are appropriate. The leper was segregated from society, reduced to an untouchable, and made to document any evidence of healing with the priestly authorities (e.g., Mark 1:40-44). For twelve years the woman with the flow of blood (Mark 5:25-34) had suffered from ritual uncleanness due to the emission of blood. Both the leper and the woman with the flow had lived outside of the mainstream of society, relegated to its margins, ostracized, and feared. Likewise, all those with deformities were suspect, because their condition meant they were less than "holy" in the Levitical sense (e.g., the man with the withered arm, Mark 3:1-6).

By his healings of such persons, Jesus effected their social reintegration. They were made acceptable to their peers and allowed to participate fully in societal life. Thus Jesus' healings represent God's concern for the physical well-being of humans but equally the divine concern for those pushed to the margins of social life. Those healings embody God's action to liberate humans from social isolation.

Second, Jesus' message of hope for the poor had social ramifications. The concern for the poor and their plight expresses a concern for a social class system that was bred and nourished by the use of power and the abuse of the helplessness of the poor by the wealthy. Jesus' care for the poor is certainly rooted in their need but is also a reflection of a concern for societal structures that perpetuate the places of the poor and the rich. Jesus' teachings envision a society in which social class distinction, particularly as it pertains to the poor, would have no place. Hence he counsels that "the poor, the maimed, the lame, the blind" should be invited to the banquet (Luke 14:12-14). His own little community of followers represented an alternative societal structure in which wealth was used for the common good of all.

MaineSeniorCollege.Org

But finally Jesus acted generally in ways that countered the social divisions of his society. Most notable is his free association with persons of any social rank (see below). Furthermore, his persistent failure to observe social custom, enforced by social ranking, is apparent. He touches the leper (Mark 1:41) and thereby violates the social and religious taboo regarding leprosy. He makes a Samaritan the hero of a parable (Luke 10:30-37) and converses with a Samaritan woman (John 4:7-26), thereby attacking head-on the hatred of the Jews and Samaritans for one another.[9] He dines with those of questionable religious purity, thereby entering into a level of intimacy that was thought to endanger his own purity (e.g., Mark 2:15-16). He treats women with dignity and equality and even includes them among his disciples (e.g., Luke 8:1-3). By doing so he smashed a social barrier that had imprisoned females in a wasteland of inferiority.

Jesus' use of the metaphor of "Father" for God, it has been argued, was in essence an assault on the authoritarian role of fathers in the structure of the household of the day. Since God is Father, no human can claim the authority of father—"call no one your father on earth, for you have one Father—the one in heaven" (Matt. 23:9). Significantly in Mark 3:34 "fathers" are not mentioned. As Elisabeth Schüssler Fiorenza has suggested, Jesus invoked the image of God as Father, "not to justify patriarchal structures and relationships . . . but precisely to reject all such claims, powers and structures . . . denying any father, and all patriarchy, its right to existence."[10] The family, the basic unit of societal structure conceived with its center in the absolute authority of the father figure, is thus dealt a fatal blow. This knockout punch to an authoritarian family structure held the promise of the liberation of women and children from the oppression of the absolute patriarchal figure.

Furthermore, Jesus' radical teachings on service and humility (e.g., Matt. 20:26) implanted an erosive substance in the very foundations of the social hierarchy of his day. It challenged the marrow of social authority. If taken seriously, this teaching threatened the very fabric of the social system with all of its oppression and injustice.

Each of these features suggests that Jesus' ministry was the beginnings of a countercultural movement. That movement systematically dismantled the social barriers that had been erected in the name of religious propriety and social order. It drove a pointed blade into the heart of the oppressive social system of Jesus' day. Jesus' role as a radical social protester has many implications for Christians today, but fundamentally it lifts the curtain surrounding the God of Jesus, enabling us to see a God who is obsessed with the welfare, most especially the social conditions, of humans.

Political Welfare

That passionate devotion to the social welfare of persons is akin to a concern of the God of Jesus for the political situation of humans. In sum, the Gospels portray a Jesus who taught and modeled a freedom from political subjugation. Jesus teaches no political theory, advances no political program, and advocates no overt political rebellion. But his ministry did reflect a political consciousness. It could be no further from the truth than to conclude that for Jesus religion and politics did not mix.

Jesus gives voice and person to the divine concern for the political welfare of humans in much the same way as he articulated and enacted a concern for social well-being. Above all Jesus modeled a sense of freedom from political oppression. He lived in such a way as to defy all political power that inhibited him. He showed only contempt for the power of Herod Antipas, even when it is reported to him that the minor royalty would have him dead. That "fox" could hold no power over Jesus (Luke 13:31-33). He refused to kowtow to the Jerusalem authorities who tried to intimidate him (Mark 7:1-8). Brought before the officials who held the power of life and death over him (or so they thought!), he refused to cooperate with them in his own trial (e.g., 14:61; 15:5). The image of the silent lamb led to its slaughter is the image most commonly associated with Jesus' refusal to defend himself at his trial (cf. Isa. 53:7). But that metaphor fails to do justice to Jesus' defiance of the injustice of the political system that victimized him. His silence is a shout of protest against all political oppression.

Again, Jesus' call to radical servanthood is an eroding of the foundations of a political system built on absolute and oppressive authority. In Mark 10:42 "those whom [the Gentiles] recognize as their rulers" and "their great ones [who] are tyrants over them" are clearly references to political leaders. In contrast to the kind of authority exercised from the seats of political power, the disciples are to assume the posture of servants. Such a teaching sets in sharp contrast the will of God for political order, on the one hand, and, on the other, a political system built on power that oppresses the weak. Again, Jesus calls for a freedom from intimidation by such power.

But does Jesus not sanction the political order by his famous statement that one should "give to the emperor the things that are the emperor's" (Matt. 22:15-22; Mark 12:13-17; Luke 20:20-26)? In a sense, yes. That answer to the devious question posed to Jesus contains a recognition of the place of political order and the proper loyalty and support of such an order. But the verse is often misunderstood and misapplied because of a neglect of its social setting. Actually the saying implies a radical defiance of political oppression, because the duality of the "things that are the emperor's" and the "things that are God's" is in no sense balanced. The saying asserts that one's ultimate loyalties are due to God, not the political system. In a political system in which the ingredients were all in place to attribute deity to the emperor Caesar, Jesus denies the political chief executive officer the main ingredient to make that move. One's final commitment is to God and the reign of God, and that radically qualifies the authority of the political system. According to this clever response, Caesar gets only the leftovers —the political order is supported only insofar as it executes the will of God and no further. Jesus' words, then, are another instance of a defiance of a political order that fails to perform its rightful service to humans. Like the Sabbath, it is made for humans and not humans for it (Mark 2:27).

The unique stories Luke includes in the account of the birth of Jesus make explicit this interpretation of the ministry of Jesus. Mary's psalm of praise (the "Magnificat") is filled with political allusions to God's actions (e.g., 1:52, "he has brought down the powerful from their thrones"). The words of Zechariah (the "Benedictus") predict the liberation of Israel through God's messianic agent: "[God] has looked favorably on his people . . . that we would be saved from our enemies and from the hand of all who hate us . . . to grant us that we, being rescued from the hands of our enemies, might serve him without fear" (1:68-74). Simeon is described as one "looking forward to the consolation of Israel" (2:25), and Anna speaks "about the child to all who were looking for the redemption of Jerusalem" (2:38). This language clearly has political overtones, for the enemies of Israel were the Romans (cf. Luke 19:43) and the "redemption" was nothing other than political liberation from the oppression the Jews experienced under Roman rule (cf. 24:21). Most certainly the evangelist Luke wanted his readers to understand the Jesus story in terms of its political impact.[11]

The Jesus image of God is, therefore, one that cares for the political welfare of humans. God acknowledges the need for political order as a means toward human fulfillment. But humans are entitled to freedom from despotic political rule, and the one who reveals God lived that freedom, in spite of the political system of his time.

Summary

Jesus also addressed the intellectual needs of humans, for instance, by teaching in the role of a rabbi of his time (e.g., Matthew 5). Furthermore, Jesus obviously addressed the spiritual needs of humans, that is, needs arising from one's interior relationship with God (e.g., Matt. 6:5-6). These are both so conspicuous that they hardly need to be argued.

What does need to be observed, however, is the holistic concern of Jesus' ministry. The human being in his or her total existence was the object of Jesus' love. Physical, emotional, economic, social, political, as well as intellectual and spiritual needs were all objects of the words and actions of Jesus. Consequently, one must conclude that the God revealed in that human life is a God who is concerned for the whole life of the divine creation. In view of the life and ministry of Jesus, the claim that God cares only for the soul of humans and acts only for the spiritual welfare of people cannot be justified. Such a claim ignores a large part of what attracted Jesus' attention and energies. More truthful is the proposal that the Jesus image of God is of one passionately devoted to human welfare in all of its various dimensions and components.

The God Who Cares for All Persons

However trite it may be to observe the universal concern of God, the truth of that observation is so important for social ministry that it must be emphasized and in even stronger terms than are usual. This is so for two reasons. First, the universalism of God's care is at the very heart of the Christian movement. Second, that universalism resides equally at the heart of Christian ministry. Jesus' ministry exemplified God's universal care within a social and religious context that made it revolutionary.

The Social and Religious Setting

It was suggested earlier that the Hebraic religion and Judaism struggled with the issue of inclusivism and exclusivism. That struggle was not resolved by the time of Jesus. Ample evidence of disagreement and debate over the issue is found in the Jewish literature of the first century C.E. Generally, Palestinian Judaism, especially in certain of its forms, was weighted toward an exclusivism. On the other hand, Hellenistic Judaism had become far more open and tolerant of others, even to the point that there was a kind of Jewish apologetic directed toward the Gentiles in writers such as Philo of Alexandria.

Furthermore, the exclusivistic tendencies of religious cleanness and holiness have already been cited in chapter 1. That tendency fashioned an exclusivism that not only limited the participation of the Palestinian Jew in gentile affairs but also restricted associations among Jews themselves. One drastic expression of this sort of intra-Jewish exclusivism is to be found in the Qumran community, a sectarian movement of Essenes devoted to purity from all that which might compromise one's standing before God. Among the writings of Qumran is to be found a passage that exemplifies a mentality of exclusivism carried to its logical extremes. In an addendum to the *Scroll of the Rule* a passage describes "the assembly of the righteous" and who shall be included in it. It prescribes the holiness of the assembly, as follows:

> And let no person smitten with any human impurity whatever enter the assembly of God. And every person smitten with these impurities, unfit to occupy a place in the midst of the congregation, and every person smitten in his flesh, paralysed in his feet or hands, lame or blind or deaf, or dumb or smitten in his flesh with a blemish visible to the eye, or any aged person that totters and is unable to stand firm in the midst of the congregation: Let these persons not enter to take their place in the midst of the congregation of men of renown, for the angels of holiness are in their congregation.[12]

This admittedly drastic view is nonetheless illustrative of a movement among some Jews of the first century in their effort to live in accord with their understanding of religious purity. Of course, life for Judaism in the first century was tenuous at best. The exclusivism that came to expression in that situation must be understood rather than condemned. It constituted an effort to preserve a people threatened with extinction. Without the tradition of exclusivism reaching back to the period following the return from exile in the sixth century B.C.E., the Jewish people might well have become absorbed into the societies of their neighbors and their tradition lost forever. In a sense, then, we are indebted to Jewish exclusivism. But exclusivism has its place only as a means of self-preservation.

The radically exclusivistic position of the Essenes was symptomatic of an extreme reliance on the imminence of the appearance of the Messiah and an excessive piety in preparation for that time. Still, it suggests to us the kind of atmosphere in which Jesus' Jewish contemporaries lived and enables us to see his inclusivism in all of its radicality.

Jesus' Radical Inclusivism

The Gospel of Mark shows how Jesus included in the compass of his care so many of those whom the Essenes excluded from their assembly. Jesus ministers to the lame (2:1-12), the blind (8:1–10), the deaf and the mute (7:31-37), and the "blemished," for instance, the leper (1:40-44) and the man with the withered arm (3:1-6). Whereas the Qumranians excluded women and children, Jesus included them in the circle of his healing (e.g., 1:39-41; 7:24-30). If the tottering elderly were viewed as unworthy to stand before God, they are honored and treated with dignity in the Gospels (e.g., Luke 2:36-38).

But the universal inclusivism of the ministry of Jesus is best illustrated by means of his associations. The Gospels report that Jesus became notorious for his free affiliations with those ostracized by others for religious, social, and political reasons. In fact he is called "a glutton and drunkard, a friend of tax collectors and sinners" because of his free associations with social outcasts (Matt. 11:19; Luke 7:34).

A list of those associations will help us comprehend the extent of his wide inclusivism. First on the list of his frequent associations were those labeled "sinners" (e.g., Mark 2:15-17; Luke 7:38; 15:1). Some debate exists as to whether this title (*hamartōloi*) was a purely religious designation or whether it denoted those guilty of serious social crimes (e.g., murder, adultery). However that is decided, the libelous title on the lips of Jesus' opponents clearly means that these are people with whom a respected leader would not associate. Yet they are common in Jesus' company, as the charges against him testify. His ministry included those who stood condemned by socioreligious norms of the time.

Tax collectors (*telōnēs*) represent the second most prominent group of associates. In first-century Palestine there was a widespread hatred and resistance to taxation. Judas's revolt in 6 C.E. was in part aimed against the taxation imposed by Rome. Foreign taxation was regarded as tribute rendered to a foreign deity, whereas it was properly

Pharisees
did not handle
coins — looked at
images

due only to God. That the land belonged to God, not to foreigners or even Jews themselves, was a long-standing Jewish conviction. Hence, the taxation of the land was especially offensive. Furthermore, the payment of Roman taxes involved the exchange of coinage. Using foreign coins with images of foreign rulers was a violation of the Jewish abhorrence of images. In strict Pharisaism to handle such coins was to defile oneself. The Romans did not respect the tax relief provided by the Sabbatical year, and hence their taxation stood in violation of the Torah. After 70 C.E. the half-shekel tax formerly paid to the temple was collected by Romans and sent to the Temple of Jupiter, adding still another demeaning offense to the whole system. Taxes were, then, a controversial issue in the first century.[13]

This hatred of the taxation naturally was transferred to the persons responsible for its collection. These persons were not only suspect in the eyes of the Jews for all the reasons just listed but were also universally despised in the Greco-Roman world because they were placed in positions rife with opportunities for fraud and misconduct.[14] Thus, when Luke has the Pharisee lump the tax-collectors in with "extortioners, unjust, adulterers," he expresses the view not only of Jews of Jesus' time but Gentiles in the evangelist's own community (Luke 18:11).

Tax collectors were businessmen who contracted to collect revenues in a prescribed area, which they leased. In turn they hired a group of individuals who exercised the actual collections. This distinction between the major figure and his army of collectors is suggested in the Gospels by the two titles, "chief tax collector" (*architelōnēs*, Luke 19:2) and the simple "tax collector" (*telōnēs*, Matt. 10:3). The first designated enterprising persons of some wealth (if not moral integrity). The second was used of individuals, many of whom were poor and of low social rank. They may have been driven to this unseemly work by sheer desperation. Their dirty work brought them only contempt and social discrimination, but it made a living.

Jesus is said to have spent a good deal of his time precisely with this despised class of workers. They came to him apparently because of his refusal to view them in the same light as did others in the society and his willingness to befriend them. He eats with them—an expression of intimacy in which he opens himself to the influence of their character (e.g., Matt. 9:10-11). He calls one of them to take a *who* place among his followers, and that one is counted among the twelve disciples (Matt. 10:3). They are numbered among the precious lost ones whom God is finding in the ministry of Jesus. The parables of the lost sheep, lost coin, and prodigal son in Luke 15 are all addressed to tax collectors and sinners (15:1). Jesus makes a tax collector the model of piety in the parable of the tax collector and the Pharisee (Luke 18:9-14) and regards the repentant actions of Zacchaeus a model of morality for Christian discipleship (19:1-10).

Jesus' radical inclusiveness violated the social and moral barriers constructed between the tax collectors and the respected of the time. The despised collectors of the taxes are embraced as objects of God's universal care.

So too are the prostitutes (*pornē*). Jesus becomes their advocate (Matt. 21:31). In Luke 7:37-50 Jesus accepts the love and gratitude of a woman who is labeled a sinner (vs. 37 and 39), and we are told that "she loved much." In all likelihood but without certainty the intention is to depict this woman as a prostitute.

The Samaritans were as despised and ostracized as were the sinners, tax collectors, and prostitutes of Jesus' time. The animosity between the Jews and Samaritans dates back to the period following the return from exile. The Jews regarded the Samaritans as "half-breeds," heretics, and religiously unclean. But the pitch of hostility between Jews and Samaritans had reached its zenith in the first century. The Samaritans had disclaimed kinship with the Jews to avoid persecution in 175 B.C.E. The Jews had later (125 B.C.E.) destroyed Samaria and its temple. Herod the Great had built a temple to Caesar in Samaria, making that land and its inhabitants even more repugnant to the Jews. Then in the early years of the first century the Samaritans had smuggled human bones into the temple in Jerusalem, defiling the most sacred of Jewish places. An incident in 48–52 C.E. entailed the murder by Samaritans of a group of Galilean Jews as they passed through a border village on their way to Jerusalem for Passover. The Jews retaliated by massacring the inhabitants of the village.

In spite of this intense hatred of the Samaritans, Jesus includes them in his ministry in several ways. The Gospel of John preserves a tradition of Jesus' conversation with a Samaritan woman, over her vocal objections, and of a period of successful ministry in a Samaritan village (4:1-42). The incident concludes with the Samaritans hailing Jesus as "Savior of the world" (v. 42). In spite of the prohibition against a mission to Samaria reported in Matt. 10:5, Luke is careful to omit such a prohibition, suggesting that the third evangelist also might have been aware of the tradition reported in John.

In the Gospel of Luke Jesus is represented as giving special prominence to the Samaritans. Jesus refuses to punish an uncooperative

Samaritan village, as his disciples desire. Their desire gives voice to the Jewish hostility toward Samaritans, but Jesus will have no part of it (Luke 9:51-56). A Samaritan, instead, appears as the hero of a parable and an example of what it means to be a neighbor (Luke 10:29-37). And a Samaritan leper exemplifies gratitude (Luke 17:11-19).[15]

In contrast to the bitterness toward the Samaritans, the compassion of Jesus encompasses them, as it does others for whom his society had only contempt.

Finally, the ministry of Jesus included women in a way that was revolutionary for the time. A summary of one view of the usual status of women in the first century both in the Greco-Roman world and among Jews is provided by Charles Carlston in a memorable passage:

> On balance . . . the picture drawn is a grim one. Women, if we were to trust the ancient wisdom, are basically ineducable and empty-headed; vengeful, dangerous, and responsible for men's sins; mendacious, treacherous, and unreliable, fickle; valuable only through their relationships with men; incapable of moderation or spontaneous goodness; at their best in the dark; interested only in sex—unless they are with their own husbands, in which case (apparently) they would rather talk. In short, women are one and all "a set of vultures," "the most beastly" of all the beasts on land or sea, and marriage is at best a necessary evil.[16]

Given this common view, it is little wonder that women were excluded from among those capable of religious and moral responses and unreliable as advocates for a religious position.

In spite of this view of women among his contemporaries, Jesus treats women with dignity and respect. He treated them no differently than he treated men and never degraded them. Instead, he is presented as one who honored women and their role. He used women as the protagonists of his parables, for instance the parables of the leaven (Matt. 13:33 and Luke 13:20-21) and the lost coin (Luke 15:8-9). Not only does this suggest that women may provide worthy models of life in the kingdom of God but also that Jesus knew and lifted up the common life of women in his day.

Women are portrayed as persons of exemplary faith in a number of cases (e.g., Mark 5:24-34; 12:41-44; Luke 7:36-50; 10:38-42; Matt. 15:21-28). Perhaps most interesting is the way the Gospel of John portrays women. The Samaritan woman of John 4 is a powerful witness to Christ, which results in her winning the faith of many in her village. Mary and Martha are presented as examples of faith, love, and gratitude (chaps. 11 and 12). Mary Magdalene is portrayed as the first apostle, sharing with others her experience of the risen Christ (20:1-18). Gender differences did not matter to Jesus.

Moreover, Jesus is an advocate for women. The story of the sinful woman who anoints Jesus in Luke 7:37-50 exemplifies this. But Jesus' rejection of the custom of divorce in his own day (Mark 10:2-9; Matt. 19:3-8) is another case of his advocacy on behalf of women. His protest against the inhumane treatment of women in the divorce process is surely one of the reasons Jesus rejects the provision that a man could divorce his wife. The deuteronomic legislation regarding divorce (Deut. 24:1-4) was widely interpreted to mean that a man could dismiss a wife for anything he regarded as indecent about her— even an act of oversalting his soup! Jesus' rejection of the legal basis of divorce was motivated, at least in part, by the injustice done to women by such practices.[17]

Moreover, that women were included among the disciples of Jesus is often argued. The issue reaches beyond the limited scope of this study, but in the Gospel of Luke it is clear that women are disciples (8:1-3). The same is true of the Gospel of John, as has already been indicated.

Obviously Jesus not only rejected the common view of women but acted in protest against it. Gender distinctions were ignored by this radical prophet, whose love reached the most lowly and despised.

We have already seen how Jesus' ministry included the poor and the afflicted, who likewise were regarded as social outcasts for religious reasons (especially, e.g., the lepers, Luke 5:12-14). To be added to the list of the groups included in the scope of Jesus' ministry were the common people (e.g., Luke 7:11; 8:40) and the criminals (e.g., Luke 23:40-43). The Jesus model of ministry is a radically inclusive one.

If Jesus' ministry bares the nature of God, we can draw but one conclusion: God is One whose concern embraces all persons without regard to their social, moral, religious, economic, or ethnic standing. A ministry that is true to the Jesus image of God, then, is one that is as fully inclusive as was the ministry of Jesus. Such a ministry does not use social status as a criterion for acceptability, as a measure of worthiness, or as a prospect for future potential. In the words of Nolan, "Solidarity with the 'nobodies' of this world, the 'discarded people,' is the only concrete way of living out a solidarity with [humanity]."[18]

And Jesus did just that. But in Jesus God demonstrated the divine solidarity with humanity in another way.

The God Who Identifies with Suffering Humanity

Still another color must be added to this portrait of the image of God revealed in Jesus of Nazareth. That Jesus expresses the concern of God for the whole person and for all persons pictures God in a way quite consistent with the major Old Testament images surveyed in chapter 1. But those Hebraic images hinted at the fact that God is not only concerned about the suffering of humans but is even identified with them in their suffering. That element emerges in a clear way in the Jesus model of God. Specifically, the identification of God with suffering humanity is found in two shades in the portrait of God in the Gospels: the ministry and death of Jesus.

In the Ministry of Jesus

Jesus not only served the poor and addressed their needs, but by his life-style as a wandering itinerant, dependent upon others for his sustenance, he identified himself with the suffering of the poor and became one with them. By his associations with the socially and religiously outcast he demonstrated solidarity with them over against the establishment of his day. By dining, for instance, with the tax collectors and sinners he identified himself with them. By touching the leper he bound his life with those suffering physical affliction and social marginalization. Thus we have ample evidence to argue that Jesus became identified with those he came to serve. Indeed, he is reported to have illustrated what it means to become a servant of others with his own life (Mark 10:42-45).

One of the unique teachings of Jesus, it is argued, is that he addressed God as *abba* ("father" but best translated "daddy" or "papa").[19] This word was a form of address preserved for the intimacy of family relationships and was even an appropriate address of one's father only by the youngest of children. But Jesus' invitation for others to address God with this term of intimacy (e.g., Luke 11:2) implied that God was identified with their needs, "felt with those who suffer," and "wanted to live in fatherly solidarity with men [and women], and wanted to use the divine power to save them."[20]

Other aspects of Jesus' teachings and life-style further demonstrate God's solidarity with the suffering. But the most vivid representation of the way in which Jesus identified himself with the needy is found in the vision of the last judgment related in Matt. 25:31-46. That passage claims that the judgment of the nations is based upon their treatment of the needy—those who suffer hunger, thirst, nakedness, sickness, and imprisonment. When the righteous are puzzled by the king's declaration that they had served him when they served their needy neighbors, the "king" announces, "Truly, I tell you, just as you did it to one of the least of these who are members of my family, you did it to me" (v. 40). Here Jesus explicitly identifies himself with the needy. He is one with those who suffer hunger, thirst, nakedness, sickness, and imprisonment.

The point here is contingent to some degree on who the family members (*adelphoi*) are in the passage. The meaning of the term is frequently debated, and some would limit its meaning to Christians or Christian missionaries to the nations. However, a number of commentators would agree that the term means humans in general and not only Christians. Elsewhere in the Gospel Matthew uses the term "brethren" not only for disciples but for others with whom the Christian is related in everyday life (e.g., 5:23, 24, 47). It seems likely, then, that the phrase "family members" reflects Christ's relationship with all humans.[21]

The impact of the point is that Christ has entangled his life with the lives of those who suffer need and want. He feels their pain and experiences their loss. Two humans who have lived together for years and who love one another deeply gradually find that their individual lives have emotionally merged into one, even though their separate identities remain intact. Their feelings are reflections of the feelings of the other in his or her suffering. Such an experience is analogous to Jesus' identification with the needy. But he claims in a more radical manner that he is one with suffering humans and that acts on their behalf are acts on behalf of Jesus himself. If Jesus identifies with suffering humans, then God must, too. God is one with the person suffering any kind of pain.

In Jesus' Death

The identification of God with suffering humanity is grounded, however, in an even more vital demonstration, namely, the cross. This point is bound inseparably with the first. The Gospel stories of Jesus make it clear that Jesus' death was at least in part due to his identification with the poor and socially rejected. This identification and the assault on the establishment it posed resulted in the death plot against Jesus. The story lines of the synoptic Gospels reflect this fact. The death plot against Jesus is a direct result of the cleansing of the temple, as Mark makes clear and Luke suggests (Mark 11:18; Luke 19:47-48). As proposed here earlier, the driving of the money changers out of the temple was an expression of Jesus' close affinity with the poor—an act of protest against the abuse of the poor by the temple establishment. At least for Mark, Jesus' identification with the poor led him to act in such a way, and that act evoked the effort to have him silenced.

The earliest Christians sensed that the meaning of the cross involved God's suffering with as well as for humanity. This dimension of the cross is represented for us in two kinds of early Christian witness to the death of Jesus.

The first of those witnesses is found in the story of the death of Jesus in the Gospels of Mark and Matthew. In the narratives of the crucifixion in these two Gospels, Jesus is reported to have cried out, "My God, my God, why have you forsaken me?" (Matt. 27:46; Mark 15:34) The authenticity of the saying is suggested by its preservation in Aramaic form—a rare occurrence in the Gospels. The saying is clearly a quotation of Ps. 22:1, but to argue that Jesus is simply reciting a psalm in the midst of his suffering as an act of typical Jewish piety is to search for the safe way out of a difficult saying.

When faced honestly, the cry of dereliction means that Jesus in the cross has so identified himself with the human experience of suffering that he senses the abandonment of God. The identification has become complete; the solidarity is perfected. In his death Jesus undergoes even the anguish of isolation, so common in the human experience of suffering (e.g., Job).

For our purposes this means that the image of God portrayed in the death of Jesus is of one whose being is married with the being of suffering humanity, so that the fullness of human suffering is shared by God. The implicit theology of the cross as it appears especially in Mark is that the reality of God is known only in the suffering of the cross. There and there alone a human is able to discern the true identity of Jesus and confess him to be "son of God" (Mark 15:39). Mark introduces the Gospel with the title Son of God (1:1), has God declare Jesus to be the divine son on two occasions (1:11 and 9:7), attributes that identification to the demons (3:11 and 5:7), and reports that Jesus claims the title for himself (14:61-62). But the only human in Mark's narrative to make this crucial confession is the centurion at the foot of the cross (15:39).[22] God is known in the reality of suffering, because God has become identified with the suffering Jesus.[23]

The second witness to this meaning of cross is found in other New Testament literature, especially the writings of Paul. One of the themes in the Pauline view of the cross is that Jesus takes on the nature of the human condition on behalf of humanity (2 Cor. 5:21; Gal. 3:13). For Paul Christ became fully identified with humanity, including that dimension of humanity susceptible to suffering.

But not just the son suffers on the cross in solidarity with humanity; God does, as well. The efforts to articulate that identity of God with Christ and Christ with humanity are not fully developed in the New Testament, but are expressed in the liturgical poetry of Phil. 2:5-11. In language that soars beyond the limitations of human conceptuality, Christ is viewed as one equal to and in unity with God (v. 6), but he "emptied himself" in order that he might be fully identified with humanity (v. 7). That process then led finally to death on the cross (v. 8). Hence, it is not alone Christ, but Christ in his divinity who suffers and dies. Christ emptied himself of all divinity that separated him from the human experience.

The identity of Christ with God is affirmed most clearly in another piece of liturgical poetry—John 1:1-18. The opening verses of that hymn make the identification of Christ with God absolute. But the Word who is God and with God becomes flesh and dwells among humans (v. 14). The Word become flesh is the Johannine way of expressing Jesus' identification with humanity. Verse 18 then declares that the human Christ is the manifestation (literally, the "exegesis") of the nature of God. The fourth evangelist goes on to narrate the story of that one who reveals the heart of God. The narrative concludes with the affirmation that God is made known in the event of the cross in which Christ suffers death and at the same time assumes his throne as king. The fourth evangelist stresses the ironic truth that the ultimate reality is known in the cross.

In New Testament thought there is a clear sense of the cross as God's identification with the suffering of humanity through the suffering of the Son. The meaning of that extreme affirmation is too great to comprehend or articulate in systematic and logical fashion. But its implications for the social ministry of the church are eloquent. God is found revealed in the suffering common to human existence. God has become bonded with the suffering of humans. Such a view suggests that Christians approach the suffering of humanity with a peculiar and revolutionary perspective. We meet our God in the suffering person. We serve our God through serving the suffering person. Our own suffering is transformed by the strange presence of the one who has been revealed in an instrument of suffering and death, the cross.

Conclusion

If we take seriously the affirmation that God is revealed to us in the life, ministry, and death of Jesus, we must deny that God is aloof, impassive, and disconnected from human life. God cares about human existence in its totality—not just the condition of the soul, but human life in its full historical reality. God cares, furthermore, about all persons, including all who by circumstance or by social ordering have been made to reside on the fringes of a society and whom society would like to subhumanize. Finally, God's care for such persons in their full humanity is expressed in God's total identification with them in their condition. Because God's care is *agapē* ("love," 1 John 4:16), the divine being has become empty to effect a complete solidarity with suffering humanity.

The Jesus image of God affirms those major images of God that surface in the reading of the Old Testament. God affirms the full historicity of human existence, passionately acts to liberate humans from the conditions of suffering, and is identified with and hence the advocate for the poor and needy. Thus by implication the Jesus image of God affirms the Old Testament picture of a God who demands justice for all people, inclusive concern for all, and social morality as a prerequisite for proper worship. The Jesus image of God points us away from what I have called the "counter-images" of God in the Old Testament—away from an exclusion of the afflicted and foreigner and away from any view of the afflicted as punished by God for their sins.

The social ministry of the church is founded on the Jesus image of God and those Old Testament images affirmed by the revelation of God in Christ. The determination to serve the social needs of humans is implanted, nourished, and brought to fruition only by that persistent biblical picture of God as one who is passionately concerned for and identified with the suffering of humanity. That image of God is the engine that drives the church into social ministry and propels it into greater and greater efforts to meet human needs. Only when the engine is in place and is finely tuned will the social ministry of the church be faithful to the revelation of God in Christ.

But the biblical images relevant to social ministry are far from complete. They are anchored in the image of God found in the pages of Scripture. That persistent image of God is the mother lode for the ministry of the church. But there are still several veins of precious ore to be mined.

Notes

1. Cf. Tannehill's discussion of this passage (*The Narrative Unity*, 60-68) and the important role it plays in the literary structure of Luke.

2. Cf. among others Boerma, *The Rich, the Poor*, 76–86; Brown, *The Birth of the Messiah*, 350–55; and Kraus, *Theology of the Psalms*, 150–54.

3. Nolan, *Jesus Before Christianity*, 23–25.

4. Stegemann, *The Gospel and the Poor*, 18–21; Schottroff and Stegemann, *Jesus and the Hope*, 6–17; Cassidy, *Jesus, Politics and Society*, 99–101; and Stambaugh and Balch, *The New Testament* 77–78 and 91–98.

5. Cf. the insightful treatment of the subject in Pilgrim, *Wealth and Poverty*.

6. Ibid., 46–47. Cf. Jeremias, *Jerusalem in Time of Jesus*, 116. Against this view cf. Hengel, *Property and Riches*, 26–27.

7. Pilgrim, 47–48.

8. Nolan, 101–6.

9. Cf. Ford, "Reconciliation and Forgiveness," cf. on this general subject Myers, *Mark's Story of Jesus*.

10. Schüssler Fiorenza, *In Memory of Her*, 150–51.

11. Nolan, 92–100.

12. "The Rule Annexe," 2:4–9. Dupont-Sommer, *The Essene Writings from Qumran*, 107–8.

13. Ford, 83–85.

14. For this point and the succeeding discussion of tax collectors cf. Schottroff and Stegemann, 7–13.

15. Ford, 88–94.

16. Carlston, "Proverbs, Maxims, and the Historical Jesus," 95–96.

17. Cf. Kysar, *The Asundered*, 42–43.

18. Nolan, 65.

19. Cf. the provocative view of Jeremias, *The Prayers of Jesus*, 11–65; *The Central Message*, 9–30; and *New Testament Theology*, 1:61–68.

20. Nolan, 80.

21. For a brief summary of the debate over the meaning of this passage and an alternative view cf. Donahue, *The Gospel in Parables*, 109–25.

22. Kingsbury, *The Christology of Mark's Gospel.*

23. Cf. Moltmann, *The Crucified God.*

3

Images of
Community
and Discipleship

[handwritten: Caring and Active God)
↳ Key theme = total condition]

The image of God as one who cares for the total condition of all humans runs through the Bible like the major theme of a great symphony. It recurs over and over. Its form sometimes varies but it always reproduces the recognizable central motif. So in the Bible that image of God is sounded in different keys and through different instruments and amounts to a masterpiece of witness and affirmation.

But a great symphony includes a number of minor themes. They elaborate the beauty of the central motif, change the focus of attention, and harmonize with the major theme. They are like the implications of the central motif, drawing forth its beauty through contrasts and elaborations. The Bible has its secondary themes as well, drawn from the major image of God.

In this and the next chapter, two of those secondary themes command our attention. They are secondary because they derive from the central theme, namely, the image of the caring and active God. The biblical images of the people of God and discipleship is the first of the two and the images of God's future for humanity is the second. They are related in that they both have to do with the community of the people of God. The future of the community and its hope are articulated in the theme of God's future. Like a great symphony, the

[handwritten margin notes: secondly / Theme]

[handwritten bottom notes: Two Minor Themes: ① Biblical image of the people of God and discipleship ② Image of God's future for humanity]

biblical witness would be vastly diminished without these two secondary themes.

How social ministry is grounded in and determined by the images of the people of God and discipleship will become clear. Our service to other persons is shaped by our conception of the nature of the Christian community and its mission. Without these conceptions of ourselves as the people of God, our ministries are deprived of their motivation and strength, for the call to care as God cares is embodied in those conceptions.

Human Agents of God's Care

As we survey the biblical material in search for what it has to say about the people of God and discipleship, two frameworks emerge. The first of these affirms the basic fact that humans are the agents of God's care for the whole person. The second is that those agents form a community that yields a witness to the world—a witness to an alternative societal structure. We found the basic images of God in the Old Testament affirmed in the ministry of Jesus. In a similar way we find these two frameworks constructed in the Old Testament and reinforced in the New Testament.

Agency in the Old Testament

God acts in history through human agency. This fundamental view is rooted in the exodus story as a corollary to the image of God as one who cares for the enslaved people. As we saw in chapter one, in the call of Moses in Exod. 3:7-12 Yahweh describes the divine sensitivities to the people's plight and the determination to alter those conditions. God has "come down to deliver them from the Egyptians, and to bring them up out of that land to a good and broad land, a land flowing with milk and honey" (v. 8). How shall God accomplish this saving act? What means shall the divine compassion use to effect the release of the people? "Come, I will send you [Moses] to Pharaoh to bring my people" (v. 10). The divine redemption is accomplished through human agency.

Moses is as surprised as we are to learn that the divine power of social and economic healing is operative through a weak and feeble human agent (v. 11). Rather than effecting the marvelous release through sheer divine fiat, God chooses to act through a human agent. Moses expresses the deference all humans feel when faced with the request to be the liberating instrument of the divine care. God does not withdraw, however, into passivity to watch the agent struggle on his own. Instead, the presence of God provides the courage and strength to fulfill the mission (v. 12).

Moses is the model of human agency for the divine care. He represents the pattern of the agency to which humans are called again and again throughout the story of Israel. In the biblical tradition he is the example to be emulated by later agents (cf. Deut. 34:10), even the Messiah himself (Deut. 18:18). The features of this model of the human agent are important, especially his task to bring to reality the conditions God seeks. God's desire for the liberation from oppression of any and every kind becomes the basis for the agent's mission.

Israel then becomes the enlargement of that agency of mission. The Israelite people as a whole have laid upon them Moses' commission to release the Hebrews from their slavery. Israel is to maintain the justice of God exhibited in the exodus event. The principle entailed in this calling of the people is articulated in the call of Abraham in which God declares that Abraham shall be a "blessing" by which "all the families of the earth shall bless themselves" (Gen. 12:2-3). The people of Israel, stemming from Abraham, shall be a source of divine pleasure for all humans. The covenant between Yahweh and the people of Israel expresses that basic principle. In Exod. 19:6 Israel is called to be "a kingdom of priests" for the whole world. As priests, they are to be the mediators between God and the people of the world. Among other things this implies they are the means by which God's care and justice are mediated to the other nations.

In the covenant all of the people are made agents of the divine care and justice in that they are commissioned to keep the law of this God (e.g., Deut. 5:1-5; 26:16-19). In chapter one above, the law was seen as an expression of God's concern for the total well-being of the people. If now the people are responsible for the keeping of that law, they have become the agents by which God accomplishes the alleviation of those conditions that continue to oppress Israel. The covenant and the law, it may be said, are the democratization of the role of the prophet Moses—every Israelite is called to be the agent by which God's care is expressed and its transforming effects accomplished. Hence, the people of God, as a community, is the called agent of God's care for the total person.

This view is not limited to the early concept of Israel but is found in the prophetic literature of a later period as well. In the prophetic insistence that the people practice justice in their relationship with one another a basic principle is implied: The people are envoys by which the care of God is expressed. Examples abound and have been alluded to in chapter one. Another example is Isa. 42:5-9, where it is said of Israel:

> I have given you as a covenant to the people,
> a light to the nations,
> to open the eyes that are blind,
> to bring out the prisoners from the dungeon,
> from the prison those who sit in darkness (vs. 6b-7).

One marvels at how in this passage the whole people are assigned a role parallel to that given Moses in his call.

Therefore, the task of agency for God's purposes among humans is not limited to a few, elected persons within the community. It is the task of the called people as a whole. If contemporary trends have resulted in the emergence of a few "experts" whose task it is to do social ministry, while the Christian community itself sits passively by, there is something terribly amiss. The task to be instruments of the divine care is everyone's task in the divine community. If God's care is to be translated into effective action among humans, it is through the whole people of God.

That fact is expressed vividly in the later image of the suffering servant of God in Deutero-Isaiah. In four passages written in a poetic style the prophet describes one who is the servant (*ebed*) of the Lord (42:1-4; 49:1-6; 50:4-9; 52:13—53:12). Among the many scholarly questions surrounding these passages, the identity of this anonymous servant is of concern to us.[1] The nominations for the identity of this mysterious figure are varied, but it seems clear that he or she was understood to be the people of Israel or a righteous remnant of that people. In Isa. 49:3 Israel is explicitly identified with the servant. It matters little if that verse was a later addition to the original servant song. If that was the case, it only means that the Hebrew people came quickly to identify themselves with the figure of the suffering servant. That being the case, we are justified in seeing the portrayal of this servant as the vision of the role of the people of God themselves.

The function of the servant described in these four passages in Isaiah is universal, that is, directed toward the nations of the world (e.g., 42:4; 49:1, 6b). The servant is God's means of bringing justice in the world (e.g., 42:1b, 4) and mediating God's salvation (49:6b). He or she is a teacher of the law, with all of its social mandates (50:4). That the servant's mission to accomplish all of this entails suffering (50:4-10) is the most difficult and distinctive of his or her features. Making it even more difficult, the servant's suffering is vicarious—the suffering of the innocent servant atones for the wrongs of the guilty (52:13-53:12). This song presents the startling way in which serving God as an agent for social justice and righteousness invariably leads to suffering, but it is a suffering conceived as a means of correcting the ills of society.

The point to be highlighted in these songs is that the suffering servant is a depiction of the suffering of Israel in her function as God's witness in the world. Israel is the means by which the divine justice is realized in the world. But such an agency role cannot be fulfilled without suffering. Just how suffering atones for sin and furthers justice remains unexpressed. But the point is clear nonetheless: The servant of God, the representative of God's care for the welfare of humanity, is one who faces suffering in the course of her/his task. For good reason, then, the earliest Christians understood the life and death of Jesus of Nazareth as a "fulfillment" of the image of the suffering servant of God.

Before leaving the Old Testament one further point must be raised, namely, the principle that God works through human agents beyond the scope of the people of God themselves. In other words, envoys for God's care are called out of humanity in general and not only from the community of the people of God. No better example of this point is found than the assertion of Deutero-Isaiah that Cyrus, the Persian general, is the agent by which God replicates the exodus event in the return of the exiles to their homeland. In Isa. 45:1 the prophet calls Cyrus God's "anointed" (*mashiach*). Even though Cyrus does not know God, God uses him to liberate the people from their bondage in exile. This proves, says the prophet, the sovereignty of God (45:3).

The point is remarkable, for it asserts the universal use of humans as instruments for God's purpose. But it is also instructive, for it suggests that God's concern for political, social, and economic well-being is expressed through those who stand outside of the community of the people of God. The church in its social ministry does well to note this faith affirmation in considering its bond with non-Christian movements for social welfare and its alliance with secular and humanistic agencies for human good.

The Old Testament is unequivocal in its affirmation that God's care for total human welfare is executed through human agents. God enlists humans as partners in the task of working to achieve liberation from all conditions that oppress and inhibit human well-being.

Agency in the New Testament

The principle that God acts through human agency also lies at the heart of the New Testament witness. Jesus is conceived as the supreme human agent of God's care. When God chose to act decisively for the transformation of the human condition, the act took the form of an agent who was at once both God and human. The Hebraic tradition is thus affirmed and magnified by the Christ event. God does not effect the reversal of human need through divine fiat but through a humble, itinerant preacher-prophet. Human agency is attested in the incarnation. God chose to act in a flesh and blood human, who was at the same time none other than God. Even when God undertakes the direct task of agency for divine purpose, God takes the form of humanity, becoming one with those who are served. God becomes agent by taking human form.

The agency theme with regard to Christ finds its fullest expression in the theology of the Gospel of John, although it is not limited to that New Testament stream of thought (e.g., Gal. 4:4, 6; Rom. 8:3). In Johannine thought Christ is most often thought of as the envoy of God (e.g., 3:16), so that Jesus frequently speaks of himself as the one sent (sometimes *pempō*, sometimes *apostellō*) by God (e.g., 5:36; 6:38-44; 8:18, 26; 10:36; 17:3, 8, 18, 21, 23, 25). The Johannine category of envoy assumes the ancient custom that the agent who is sent by a royal figure carries the authority of the one who sent him or her. Consequently, the response to Jesus is conceived as a response to God (e.g., 5:42-47).

For the fourth evangelist Christ is God's agent sent among humans to effect their salvation. But the sending of the believers is modeled after that divine sending of the son, as John 20:19-23 indicates (and to which we will return in the conclusion). In that passage the commissioning of the disciples (in John that means all believers) is related in potent simplicity. Within that commissioning come the words of v. 21: "As the Father has sent me, so I send you." The agency task of the believing community is parallel to and modeled after the agency of Christ himself. The profundity of that concept is hardly comprehensible. Clearly, however, Jesus is sent by God out of the divine love

(3:16) and serves God through faithfulness to that love (15:9). The mission of the community of believers is likewise an expression of the divine love and is an agency of love.

This means that the mission of the church, as it is conceived by the earliest Christians, cannot be separated from the love of God revealed in the Christ event. That love gives rise to the sending of the church, even as it gave rise to the sending of Christ, and constitutes the content of the mission of the Christian community, even as it constituted the mission of Christ. From our discussion of the images of God in both the Old and New Testaments we know that that divine love is a care for the whole person and for all persons. Hence, the church knows its mission and the nature of its social responsibility from what it knows of the God who sent Christ and who now sends the church into the world.

The agency task of the community of faith is clear in the role and function of the disciples described elsewhere in the New Testament. One passage particularly important for our purposes is found in the sending of the seventy narrated in Luke 10 (cf. Matthew 10). In the early verses of that chapter Jesus gives instructions to the seventy. Those instructions include specifically what they are to do in the villages they enter. They are to "cure the sick who are there, and say to them, 'The kingdom of God has come near to you' " (v. 9). The mission of the seventy is twofold: to act and to proclaim. Notice that the healing of the physical ailments of people is given primary place but that this healing ministry is not separable from the proclamation of the good news that the reign of God has been inaugurated among them.

Luke 10:9 is important for us for several reasons: First, it highlights the fact that the ministry of the seventy is not to differ significantly from that of Christ's own ministry. As Jesus addressed the total welfare of humans in his healings (cf. chap. two), so the disciples are to do the same. The mission of the seventy is not alone to address the spiritual needs of the villagers apart from their physical conditions. Second, this command illustrates for us the way in which acts of social healing are intertwined with the proclamation of the gospel. Healing is not to be isolated from proclamation, nor proclamation from healing. Surely this commissioning of the seventy casts serious doubt on any effort to isolate what the contemporary church would call evangelism from social ministry (cf. chap. 6 below). The two are one and the same in that they are both addressed to the whole welfare of humans. They are not separable, for healing assumes the new age of

God's rule which has dawned in Christ's ministry and gives evidence of the power of that new age. Furthermore, there is no basis here in the commissioning of the seventy for the elevation of one mode of ministry over the other. Healing is not ranked above proclamation in importance, nor proclamation above healing. They are both equal and indispensable expressions of the Christ event.

But the return of the seventy, narrated in Luke 10:17-20, is equally important to our understanding of the agency of God entrusted to Christian believers. They return to Jesus amazed at and joyful over the power they have experienced: "Lord, even the demons are subject to us in your name!" Moses was promised the presence of God in his mission and experienced the power of that presence in what he was able to do on behalf of God's liberating plan. Now Jesus' disciples have a similar experience. As Jesus empowers the disciples with the Holy Spirit when they are sent out (John 20:22; Luke 24:48-49; Acts 2:1-40), so the seventy have been empowered by their master.

In Luke 10:18 Jesus depicts the significance of what the seventy representatives of his ministry have accomplished, when he declares that in their acts of healing and proclamation the forces of evil have been dethroned: "I watched Satan fall from heaven like a flash of lightning." The forces of evil, not the will of God, are expressed in the afflictions humans suffer. As those afflictions are overcome through the ministry of the seventy, the power of evil is neutralized and made impotent. The agency of humans sent by God to serve the total human welfare has cosmic effects. It alters the nature of the whole universe in altering the conditions of individual humans in their afflictions.

The pattern established in the work of the seventy finds replication in the work of the church described in the Book of Acts. Everywhere throughout the Acts of the Apostles there is evidence of, first, the power for healing invested in the church, second, the unity of healing and proclamation, and, third, the ramifications of those acts. One example will make these three points clear. In Acts 3:1-10 Peter and James heal a man who was born lame. They are instruments of God's concern for an affliction that has marred a human life and are empowered to effectuate such a healing. But then Peter uses the occasion to announce the significance of what has been accomplished (vs. 12-26). Proclamation accompanies healing. The concern for the physical affliction of the lame man is not separable from the concern for the total welfare of all the people, and Peter calls on them to repent (v. 19). Acts 4:4 suggests the results of this event in claiming that the number of believers grew. This pattern is repeated throughout the Book of Acts (e.g., 4:14; 8:7; 10:38; 28:10).

We should beware of two false assumptions that may weaken the relevance of these themes. The first is that the early church and the first disciples in particular were empowered to heal in a way in which the contemporary church is not. This assumption denies the existence of healing power in the contemporary community of faith, and supposes a narrow view of the way in which God empowers the church. God's healing power is not limited to the extraordinary act of effecting a cure immediately by touch or word. Less miraculous means of healing are also the empowerment of the Spirit. For example, in the church's advocacy for research on AIDS it brings the empowerment of God to bear on that terrible human affliction. As the church overcomes the hunger of humans in the world, it expresses the empowerment of God as surely as did Peter and John. If we limit our social ministry to the kind of healing that can be effected through the miracle of faith, however real that kind of healing may be, we limit God's means of overcoming human affliction.

The second assumption is that the healings worked by the early church were only a means to accomplish a spiritual mission. That is, it may be thought that the healings of the early church were wonders to attract attention to the church. They are only a means toward a spiritual goal, and the healing itself does not count as the accomplishment of the divine mission. That assumption is refuted by the biblical witness. The mission of the people of God, in both their biblical and contemporary forms, is to address the needs of humans on both the physical and the spiritual level.

Summary

The score for the first of the secondary themes of the biblical symphony is clearly written. Humans emerge as the agents of God's care for the total welfare of people. We are the instruments for God's love to reach the physical, social, economic, and political, as well as the spiritual, conditions of others. God does not choose to work alone. God creates co-workers—partners—in the divine enterprise. The agents never misunderstand their role and their function. Their mission is ours by virtue of having been the objects of God's care and of having been called and sent by the divine Carer. The power for our mission, therefore, is not our own but God's. And like an executive corporate officer,

God delegates authority and power to the partners of the firm in order that its mission might be accomplished.

To be the people of God, called and set apart by the graciousness of a loving Creator and Redeemer, means to become instruments of that grace and love. It is to experience both the privilege of being loved and the responsibility of that love.

The People of God As an Alternative Community

But the fulfilment of that agency to which the people of God are called entails more than individual and corporate actions on behalf of others. The witness of the community to the care of God for the total human welfare is found in healing and proclamation, in liberation and serving, and in caring and providing. But the biblical record points to another kind of testimony to the care of God, namely, the witness of the community as an alternative to the norms and structure of the society in which it finds itself.

The concept of the people of God as an alternative community means that the group functions within its society as a subculture. It is a society within a society, a minority group within the majority. It embraces and lives a different life-style from that of the general culture. The community is a counterculture in the sense that its life-style expresses values that stand opposed to those of the general culture. It must then stand over against the generally accepted norms of its day and time. It is furthermore an intentional culture in the sense that it consciously embraces and lives these different values as a means of effecting the life of the total culture. The people of God are deliberate, conscious, and purposeful in their effort to propagate their own norms for societal life to those outside the circle of their community of faith. They execute that fertilization through careful attention to what the character of their own communal life says to the society of which they are a part.

In this sense the biblical community is consistently portrayed as an alternative culture. That portrayal stretches again from Moses to Paul, from Israel to the Christian church. Our brief survey of the matter is intended to suggest the way in which the communal life of the people of God comprised a vital part of its witness to the care of God for the whole person and for all persons.

The Alternative Community in the Old Testament

Israel is formed as an alternative community from its origins in the exodus.[2] Israel stood over against the Egyptian culture as a minority subculture. Moses cultivated a sense of the distinctiveness of Israel from the Egyptians. Israel was the object of the concern of the great "I Am" who had sent Moses to execute their liberation. The Passover story told with attention to vivid detail and shaped by liturgical interests exemplifies the distinctiveness of the Hebrew people (Exodus 12). The formation of the Hebrew people from among the ʿApiru (cf. chap. 1) in bondage in Egypt involved shaping them into a distinctive, peculiar people whose difference from their culture was rooted in their affiliation with the liberating God of the exodus enterprise. That affiliation meant that the God of justice stood in criticism over the systematic oppression of humans in the name of the welfare of the empowered few of the Egyptian society.

The alternative nature of the Hebraic community as the people of God is summarized in the covenant. Israel is called to be a "holy nation" (Exod. 19:6; cf. Deut. 26:19). They are set apart from the society in which they live. They are God's community, formed by divine act and subject to divine rule. As such they are a means by which God reaches the nations of the world. Their community was an evangelical one in that they are the means of spreading the truth of this caring God who is opposed to the oppression of human life.

In no less a significant way the law defined Israel as an alternative community. While it is true that the laws reflect some of the practices of Israel's neighbors (e.g., compare the Code of Hammurabi), in their insistence on social justice the legal materials describe a society in which the care of the needy takes priority over achievement and possession (cf. chap. 1). Even the land in which the people dwell is not to be conceived of as their own, for it is God's (e.g., Lev. 25:23).[3]

Such an alternative consciousness continued in Israel's life in Canaan. Israelites again constituted a minority subculture within the Canaanite society. They stood apart because of their bond with the God who had led them out of Egypt. So, they could not serve the *Baalim* of the Canaanites and remain faithful to their Liberator (e.g., Judg. 2:11). Their worship of the God they had known in the course of their history repudiated the fertility gods of their farmer-neighbors the Canaanites. They were persistently called to their distinctive witness as Yahweh's people. Elijah's sense of loneliness on Mount Horeb illustrates the consciousness of the faithful believer over against the forces of the culture at large (1 Kings 19:14).

Indeed, the prophetic movement provides a clear example of the recurring call to a different consciousness throughout most of the Old Testament. In opposition to the royal consciousness that arose with David and persisted thereafter, the prophets spoke out for Israel's commitment to the care of God for all persons whatever their condition. In the story of Nathan and David the king supposes that it is within his power to claim for his own that which belongs to a lowly Hebrew soldier. David's act of abuse of his power nearly succeeds until the prophet Nathan encounters him and declares, "You are the man" (2 Samuel 11 and 12). Nathan is a spokesperson for a different consciousness than that of the king. It is a consciousness shaped by the character of the God of Israel. David's consciousness is, on the other hand, shaped by the human desire for power and possession. Nathan insists that the people of God counter the way that power is used to abuse the powerless.

The prophetic protest against the royal consciousness and its expression of the consciousness of the people of God as a just and caring community is witnessed in other figures as well. Elijah cannot tolerate Ahab's dispossession of Naboth (1 Kings 21), nor can Micaiah sanction the power play of Israel and Judah against Syria (1 Kings 22). In a political move Elisha commissions Jehu to take control of the monarchy and correct its abuses (2 Kings 9). The story continues with the classical prophets of the eighth through the sixth century in their persistence against the monarchy and other powerful rulers (cf. chap. 1).

From Moses through Ezekiel the prophetic movement involved the effort to prevent the demise of that distinctive consciousness of the people of Israel as a community committed to human justice founded on divine justice. It was a movement to keep the sense of the alternative consciousness of the people from giving way to the mentality of monarchy and power common among Israel's neighboring nations. As Walter Brueggemann has said, it was a movement to both criticize and energize. It criticized the compromising of that alternative status—that different consciousness rooted in the people's relationship with God—by those who fell victim to the cultural values of their day. It energized in the sense that it motivated a rejuvenation of that alternative consciousness.[4]

The suffering servant of Deutero-Isaiah pictures Israel as an alternative community, testifying to God's truth over against the societal norms of the time. Israel represented in the servant songs is conceived of as the means by which humans can exert influence in the larger society for justice and righteousness. Even its suffering in doing so (see above) is part of the means by which its agency function is fulfilled. The assumption is that the alternative community can be a means of effecting change, of being "a light to the nations" (Isa. 49:6).

Criticism of the exclusivistic movement in Israel and its effect of narrowing the concern for God to the chosen people alone notwithstanding, we must recognize that the movement for the exclusion of others in part arose as an effort to preserve what was distinctive about Israel as God's agent for an alternative community. The easy inclusion of others in the community threatened to dilute the unique values that defined the people of God. The exclusivistic movement perhaps went too far in its zeal for the cause; it tended in its later form to define the alternative community not in terms of values and distinctive consciousness but in terms of ethnic origin. Nevertheless, its roots may well have been in an understanding of Israel as a peculiar community in the world for the purpose of witness to its God.

This image of the people of God as an alternative community standing alongside while within another culture emerges again and again in the Old Testament literature. It comes to define the people, to identity them as people called by God. It is furthermore their witness to the God by whom they have been called and liberated. Their life together, in other words, points beyond themselves to the one who formed them into community. Their communal existence is a light that enlightens the nations—a beacon directing others to this God.

The Alternative Community in the New Testament

The witness of the New Testament does not significantly differ in this matter. Jesus formed a community around himself that served as an alternative to the society of his time. It was a community comprised, in large part, of the poor and the outcast, including women, tax collectors, and those called sinners (cf. chap. 2). That community existed in solidarity with the poor and their cause, and it was marked by a singular commitment to voluntary poverty and simplicity of lifestyle (e.g., Luke 10:4).

John Howard Yoder's summary of the characteristics of the community of Jesus' disciples helps us see their role as a living alternative to the society of their time.

There are thus about the community of disciples those socio-logical traits most characteristic of those who set about to change society: a visible structured fellowship, a sober decision guar-anteeing that the costs of commitment to the fellowship have been consciously accepted, and a clearly defined life style distinct from that of the crowd.[5]

The disciples constituted, therefore, a corporate body with a clear sense of self-identity as distinct from the cultural values that sur-rounded them. Moreover, there is about the corporate body of disciples a social intentionality.

Matthew characterizes the nature of the Christian community as a peculiar form of "righteousness" (*dikaiosynē*) exceeding that of the most righteous of the culture (Matt. 5:20). In what we call the Sermon on the Mount Matthew has Jesus explicate that righteousness (5:21—6:27). If in our day righteousness has come frequently to mean a spiritual matter expressed in certain acts of piety, we should be re-minded of the social dimension of righteousness in Matthew's witness to Jesus (e.g., Matt. 5:21, 24, 38). But further on Matthew portrays the righteousness demanded by discipleship in terms of "fruits" of a life (e.g., 7:16; 12:33)—the acts that comprise a life. Nor should we forget the importance attached to behavior in relationship to others in Matthew's vision of God's judgment (e.g., 25:31-46).

Matthew's sense of the word "righteousness" retains its original association with justice (*dikē*). It is out of a concept of justice in legal, political, and ethical matters that righteousness grew to take on a broader meaning. In the Septuagint the Greek word for righteousness was used to translate *sedaqah*, Hebrew for "justice." The New Tes-tament in general, and Matthew in particular, continues to conceive of the righteousness that characterizes the Christian in terms of justice in human relationships.

That kind of righteousness distinguished the Christian commu-nity, making it a community that embraced values quite different from that of the society in which it was born. A concern for the rightness of relationships marks the Christian community as an alternative community.

The Acts of the Apostles represents the church as an alternative community in unquestionable terms. Although Luke's portrayal of the earliest Christian community may be idealized, it is nonetheless an example of what it meant to be the people of God in Christ. Most important about Luke's picture of the earliest church is his insistence that it was a community in which physical need was cared for. In describing the church as it emerged after Pentecost, Luke even claims that the first Christians practiced communal ownership of property: "All who believed were together and had all things in common; they would sell their possessions and goods and distribute the proceeds to all, as any had need" (2:44-45). Out of their togetherness in Christ, there arose among the early Christians a sense that fulfillment of need took precedence over possession. The violation of that principle was the most serious of offenses against God, as the story of Ananias and Sapphira suggests (5:1-6). Furthermore, when the needs of widows were ignored, provisions were made for them (6:1-6).

That Luke understood this communal life to be an effective witness to the society in which the church lived is suggested by the way he speaks of conversions to the faith aroused by the life of the community (e.g., 2:47; 6:7). The alternative community formed by Christian believers attracted others and pulled them away from the societal values with which they lived.

Paul, in no less a way, conceived of the church as a different community set apart from its culture and witnessing to what it meant to live together as the body of Christ. He gives great attention to the necessity of meeting the needs of the poor in the community and the solidarity of the congregations of the church. In 2 Corinthians he urges liberal giving to help the poor in the congregation in Jerusalem (chaps. 8–9). A similar appeal is found in 1 Cor. 16:1-4 and Rom. 15:25-27. So important is the offering of the gentile churches for the poor of the Jerusalem congregation that Paul delays his mission to Spain in order to deliver it personally to the Christians of that city (Rom. 15:28). Paul believed that support of the poor was the common obligation laid on both the Jewish and the gentile Christians of the church (Gal. 2:10).

For Paul the church was an alternative community in the sense of its solidarity that gave expression to a concern for the poor in any part of the church. But perhaps even more important was his vision of the church as a community in which differences were transcended in Christ. The classical expression of that vision is Gal. 3:28: "There is no longer Jew or Greek, there is no longer slave or free, there is no longer male and female; for all of you are one in Christ Jesus" (cf. 1 Cor. 12:13; Col. 3:11; Eph. 6:8; 1 Pet. 1:23-25). Paul may not have always consistently pursued this vision in the advice he gave the congregations to which he wrote. Nonetheless, his vision of the body of Christ was central to his faith and stood in contradistinction to the societal norms of his day in the Greco-Roman world.

This is a vision of a community in which the ethnic origin, the social status of free or bond, and the gender distinction of persons are essentially irrelevant. The society of the church was a single, seamless fabric by virtue of its shared baptism in Christ in a day when the distinction between Jew and Gentile was a chasm in humanity, especially from the perspective of the Jews. Yet Paul's conception of the gospel was that it annihilated such a distinction. Indeed, his now famous view of "justification by faith" (e.g., Rom. 3:19-26; Gal. 2:15-16) was intended more to overcome ethnic distinctions than it was to put aside the law as a means of salvation (see chap. 6 below).[6] Because the Christ event was salvific for all humanity, the societal differentiation between Jews and Gentiles was of no significance. Thus Paul understood the community of Christ as a society that presented an option to that sharp delineation of humans according to their ethnic origin.

Further, J. P. M. Walsh argues that the Pauline concept of justification "must be understood in the light of Israelite and Jewish convictions about *sedeq* [justice]." Its communal dimension defines the identity of a group and has to do with

> an entire way of life: the way people dealt with one another, in politics and economics and work, the whole network of relationships that constitutes the life of a people. Yahweh's "justice" was to be the measure and the animating principle of Israelite life. . . . So the question of "being justified" is not simply a matter of "righteousness." It is a question about how Yahweh's purpose can be made a reality.[7]

Similarly, the social distinction between the slave and the free was overcome in the Christian community. Thus all social status was annihilated and all were equal before God and within the community. The most desired human condition—freedom—and the most dreaded—slavery—made no difference within the church. Likewise, the low estate of women in the Greco-Roman world (see chap. 2) was eliminated, so that men and women stood on equal ground within the body of Christ. Their life together was an effort to activate a principle upon which the church was founded and which is attributed to Peter in Acts 10:34: "God shows no partiality."

About these three categories of the cultural, social and sexual structures of society Richard Longenecker observes:

> It was in these areas that the early Christians faced their greatest problems socially, realized something of the significance of the gospel for their situations, and attempted to work out the implications of the gospel for their own day. The early Christians knew themselves to be "a kind of firstfruits" of God's new creation . . . and so sought . . . to be God's people in truth and practice.[8]

Paul and other New Testament writers understood the distinctiveness of the Christian community in its environment as a "holiness" (e.g., Rom. 12:1; 1 Thess. 3:13; 4:7; 1 Cor. 2:12; Heb. 12:10, 14). In doing so, they continued the Old Testament theme that viewed the people of God as called to a holiness characteristic of their God. The holiness demanded of them was a peculiar morality and yielded a communal life quite different from the established patterns of the culture.

The witness of James to the character of the Christian community also suggests an alternative society. The Letter of James takes as one of its special emphases the mandate that there shall be no partiality within the church. The author insists, first, that ethical actions are integral to Christian faith (e.g., 1:22, 27; 2:14-26), then urges the impartial and equal treatment of all persons in the church without regard to their economic status (2:1-9). In fact social status is reversed as a result of the gospel, the author claims (1:9-11; 2:5; 4:6, 10). The physical needs of persons are equal in importance to their spiritual needs (2:15-16; cf. 5:14-15). The result is that James envisions a community in which a full equality is enjoyed by all, especially without distinction as to one's economic status.

Finally, the peculiar perspective of the Gospel of John evidences a sense of the Christian community as an alternative to the culture of its day. The fourth evangelist articulates the view that the church is an alien society in the world, and the world is considered the realm of unbelief, rejection, and evil. Jesus himself is the stranger in a foreign land who descends into that evil territory to reveal God and then once again ascends to his otherworldly home. The Johannine Christians understood themselves in the light of their view of Christ. Therefore, they were not of the world and felt isolated from their environment (e.g., John 17). Still, they are sent into that foreign world to minister to it.[9]

The Johannine perspective is radical—even sectarian—in its seclusion of the church from the world. Yet it presents the way in which the church stands over against the world, even while the church is called to service in the world. In a day in which the tendency may be to identify the church and American culture too closely, the Gospel of John is a salutary antidote. The church cannot accommodate itself to the culture without losing its distinctive role as a witness to God's will.

Summary

The New Testament, like Old, depicts the people of God as an alternative community. The life the church has in Christ transforms the character of their communal existence. It produces a community marked by a distinctive righteousness, intent upon the care of the needy within their circle, and committed to an equality quite unlike the practice of the culture in which the church resided. It is a communal life evoked by the nature of the act of God in Christ—an act that gives expression to a God who "shows no partiality" and who is passionately committed to the needy. Their life together expresses their faith as truly as do their verbal confessions; their life together witnesses to the gospel as clearly as do their proclamations.

Through the church as the alternative community, then, God seeks the dissemination of the good news that a new age has begun—an age that marks a new possibility for human social life. Human sin created the necessity of a divided humanity. God's redeeming act in Christ gives birth to the prospect of a new humanity, united and living at peace with one another. In the words of Ephesians, Christ "is our peace, in his flesh he has made both groups into one and has broken down the dividing wall, that is, the hostility . . . that he might create in himself one new humanity in place of the two" (2:14-15).

Conclusion

In summary it is clear that the biblical witness calls Christians to be agents of divine care in the world. Through our actions on behalf of others we are the bearers of God's care to the society of which we are a part. But the biblical witness also lays upon the community of the people of God a necessity that we be an alternative community, standing as a testimony to the kind of societal life God desires for humans. Agency for the divine care for the total welfare of all people is a matter of being as well as behavior. By its example, the church makes its witness to the world and offers a critique of those values that divide people and allow for the oppression of many to the benefit of a few.

The alternative community the Bible describes, then, has a number of features. First, it is formed by the character of the God who has acted to bring the community into existence. The justice and care of God become expressed in a community that practices that justice and care. Second, the community formed by this God, therefore, is committed to a set of values that stands in opposition to those embraced by the society of which the community is a part. The community of God's people is ruled by the God who has formed them, and the divine values take precedence over social norms, customs, and mores. Third, that alternative set of values modeled in the community calls into question what the society values and practices. It functions, in other words, as a judgment of the cultural values of the day.

But, fourth, it also offers the culture an option—another way of life to that which is the norm. Hence, the alternative witness of the people of God is a call to freedom. The community proclaims in its life together that humans can be freed of the pressures to conform to societal values and to perpetuate the established powers. Finally, in that call to freedom implicit in the life of the community there is a call to faith in the God whose liberating actions are embodied in the people of God. With such a call to faith the people of God complete their witness to the one to whom they owe their lives and freedom.

Needless to say, the contemporary church knows the struggle between the community life implicit in the gospel and the norms of its society. That struggle is a persistent one that is not easily resolved. But the resolution of that struggle lies at the heart of what it means for the church to have a social ministry. For without the foundation of a community that gives expression to God's liberating care and justice, the efforts of the church to minister beyond its own membership do not maintain credibility. To nurture a community that is an alternative to the power structures of the world, to the indifference of modern life, and to the inequality of relationships on which society is based is to fuel the engines of social ministry. In the words of Hendrik Berkhof, "We shall only resist social injustice and the disintegration of community if justice and mercy prevail in our own common life and social differences have lost their power to divide."[10]

The witness of the alternative community is one dimension of the responsibility of the people of God as agents of the divine liberation. The acts of God's human agents for the needy and oppressed comprises the other dimension of that responsibility. Together they round out the full task of a people called to be the means by which the care of God becomes channeled into the world.

But the church lives with an eye focused on the future, even as it lives out of the history of the past and attends to the present. That future dimension of the life of faith will be examined in the next chapter.

Notes

1. On this question and the servant songs in general, cf. the classical discussions in Mowinckel, *He That Cometh*, 187–260; Rowley, *The Servant of the Lord;* and North, *The Suffering Servant.*

2. Much of this discussion is based on the insights of Brueggemann in his brilliant book, *The Prophetic Imagination*, although it is expressed in different ways. Cf. the very useful discussion from a more conservative position in Mott, *Biblical Ethics and Social Change*, chap. 7.

3. Cf. Brueggemann, *The Land.*

4. Brueggemann, *The Prophetic Imagination*, chaps. 3 and 4.

5. Yoder, *The Politics of Jesus*, 46–47.

6. Cf. Stendahl, *Paul among Jews and Gentiles* and Dahl, "The Doctrine of Justification."

7. Walsh, *The Mighty from Their Thrones*, 157.

8. Longenecker, *New Testament and Social Ethics*, 94.

9. Kysar, *John.*

10. Berkhof, *Christ and the Powers*, 42.

4

Images of
the Future
(re: Bible)

Christians are pilgrims whose past has energized a journey, the destination of which lies in the future. So we are a people whose vision is divided. We look, on the one hand, to the past, for it is in the past that God has acted to redefine who we are and whose we are. On the other hand, we look into the future in anticipation of the completion of God's actions in our world, for there is a sense in which God's reign among us is still imperfect. This split vision that characterizes the Christian people is determined by the biblical witness itself. The Bible too is split in its vision, pointing consistently to the past while also beckoning into the future.

The future about which the Bible speaks is the subject of this chapter. The eschatological dimension of the biblical witness is widely recognized. It permeates nearly every stratum of the biblical material, like a counteraction to the narratives of the past. What is not so frequently recognized, however, are the implications of this future dimension of the Bible for social ministry.

Those implications are important for at least two reasons. The first is that the description of the future promised by God in the pages of the Bible contains important insights into what God desires for humanity. The eschatological visions dotting the biblical testimony are snapshots of the conditions God wills to bring into being for creation. They are, therefore, additional instances of the care of God

79

for human welfare. Furthermore, they make that divine care specific in describing the concrete situation God holds out for us.

Social ministry finds in those biblical images of the future the kind of life to be sought for ourselves and others. The eschatological visions are God's goals for the future and, therefore, become goals for our ministry in serving others. Not that the church's social ministry "brings the kingdom of God" or even aspires to do so. That well-intentioned motivation for social ministry is fraught with serious theological problems. The eschatological goal of the divine plan is finally brought about by God and God alone, and we dare not pretend that our puny efforts can achieve it. But the visions of the future enlist our efforts. They invite our participation and motivate our ministry. The principle of human-divine cooperation discussed in the previous chapter mandates that we seek what God seeks. In sum, the eschatological visions provide social ministry with its direction and goal.

2. The second reason for studying these visions of the future is that hope energizes activity. Hopelessness, on the other hand, fuels passivity. For instance, so long as we believe that there is no possibility of achieving world peace—if only for a time—there is no reason to act on behalf of world peace. Hope delivers possibility, and possibility excites action. Only a people with a vision of what is possible will devote themselves to working toward the realization of that possibility.

Social ministry runs on the fuel of possibility. The coals of social hopelessness smolder within contemporary America. The problems of our society seem hopelessly complex and the solutions unrealistically optimistic. We Christians are tempted to acquiesce to such hopelessness—to retire to resignation and to abdicate responsibility to the "experts" who understand complex problems. The biblical visions of the future offer an antidote to such hopelessness and passivity. They describe a future that is possible through faith and claim that God is committed to actualizing that possibility. They are visions of a future not only endorsed by God but promised by God. They cut through the lethargy of despair and transplant expectation for acquiescence.

But do the biblical visions of the future not encourage passivity insofar as they claim the future is entirely of God's doing? There is a paradoxical character to those promises of the future. It is true they are often couched in language that suggests that God alone is responsible for their realization. But they are intended not alone as promises to a helpless people but as empowerment. The vision of the future in the Revelation of John, for instance, is the promise of God to Christian communities faced with opposition far beyond their power to conquer. Yet John of Patmos does not urge the persecuted Christians to succumb to the opposition but to resist it with all their might with the power they have—the power of their faith. The point is that the eschatological visions of the future are misunderstood when they are read as a rationale for inactivity. They recruit human cooperation, even as they attribute the future to God's work alone.

This discussion therefore needs to address the biblical visions of a God-willed future with an eye toward how they relate to the congregation's ministry to society. The survey will begin with visions found in the Old Testament and conclude with those in the New Testament. The basic unity of the Bible will be reconfirmed by the coherence of the Old and New Testaments on yet another issue.

The Future in the Old Testament

Jürgen Moltmann has spoken of the "overspill" of promise in the biblical witness. He means by this the fact that in the history of Israel the fulfillment of promise always entails additional promise. Therefore, the final fulfillment is never attained in the pages of the Bible but always stands in the future. He interprets this biblical process with these words:

> the reason for the overplus of promise and for the fact that it constantly overspills history lies in the inexhaustibility of the God of promise, who never exhausts himself in any historic reality but comes "to rest" only in a reality that wholly corresponds to him.[1]

Indeed, biblical history could be written in just such terms. God promises, the promise is fulfilled, a new promise is given, it is fulfilled, another given, and so forth. Israel's history is just so. In fact, in the Old Testament we find one promise-fulfillment after another leading all the way from Abraham to the Book of Daniel. That history will be sketched here and some of its meaning for social ministry extracted. The journey through the Old Testament will be divided into two of the classic groupings of the literature: Torah and Prophets.

Promise-Fulfillment in Torah

There are two promises and fulfillments that pervade the first five books of the Old Testament: the promises to Abraham and Sarah and those to the people of Israel. The roots of Israel's understanding of its history are found in God's promise to Abram and Sarah. They are promised two of the symbols of a full human life—land (e.g., Gen. 12:1) and descendants (e.g., Gen. 15:1-6; 17:15—18:15). Discussion of land will await exposition of the place it plays in the call of Israel out of Egypt and into Canaan. But the role of descendants in Abram's future is important here. Abraham and Sarah's predicament of childlessness must be seen in the context of their time and Hebraic mentality. To be without an heir was to be without a future; it was condemnation to the past. The future was experienced through one's heirs, and children were one's contact with and involvement in a future.[2]

God promises a future to Abraham and Sarah by means of children, even though they despair of such a future. The promise is not simply or even primarily the enjoyment of a family but rather the prospects of a future. God betrays in these ancient stories a desire to give humans possibilities for their lives. The legendary promise to Israel's forbearers is paradigmatic of the divine promise of future to all humans. We are not intended by God to live futureless, but with the prospects of what time might hold. To this end, then, all of the visions of the future in the biblical material are intended as God's gift of a future and the endowment of possibility for human life. The early stories of Sarah and Abraham anticipate the whole biblical emphasis on the future and its assurance that humans are not left bereft of expectation.

The church's social ministry aims at the task of carving a future out of despair and of furnishing anticipation. The ministry to the elderly, for instance, not only offers assurance of life beyond death but nourishes the possibilities of this life, even for those for whom there seems to be little time left. God's gift of children to the elderly and childless Abraham and Sarah did just that.

Abraham and Sarah are also promised land. The promise to Israel is similar—they shall possess a land for themselves after their rescue from the oppression of slavery in Egypt. The exodus story is filled with that promise (e.g., Exod. 3:8; Lev. 20:24; Num. 14:8; Deut. 6:18). The reminders of the gift of their land function in many ways in the material of the Pentateuch, but what interests us is the implication of that promise of land.

Land suggests the importance of place and belonging for human existence. God is concerned in this case that humans have a setting for their lives—so that life will not be lived without the specificity of roots in a locale. Abraham and Sarah were entitled to "a place to call their own." The Israelite slaves were called to freedom, but freedom without a homeland would be meaningless. The divine will is that people have a sense of belonging to place as well as to time. It is not accidental that the theology of the Torah claims that humans are made from the "dust from the ground" (Gen. 2:7) and then are promised a land in which they may dwell. As materiality is integrally part of the conception of the human creature in Genesis 1 and 2 (see chap. 1 above), humans need material place in order to experience the fullness of their existence. We are creatures of place and need locus in which to mature. The issue addresses the basic human sense of homelessness, as Brueggemann has perceived.[3]

The social ministry of the church recognizes that God desires place and home for human existence, and the church is committed to seek the fulfillment of that divine desire. That commitment entails a ministry to the elderly who are often deprived of their homes and to all the homeless of our society. The determination to provide "land" for humans necessitates the provision of shelter, but moreover seeks to overcome all that which makes a person's "land" less than God desires. An oppressive home—one filled with dictatorial authority or physical abuse—is not the "land flowing with milk and honey" God desires. The church is committed to achieving a "good land" for all people. That commitment leads us from concerns for the street people of our society, to fair housing for minority groups, and to action on behalf of blacks living under apartheid.

In the case of each of the major promises of the Torah God is faithful in the promise. Sarah and Abraham become the parents of an entire nation. The land promised to them and their descendants is finally given in the conquest and settlement of Canaan. But the fulfillment of the promise spills over into the future with additional promise.

Promise-Fulfillment in Prophets

The second major division of the Old Testament is the Prophets, including not only the literary prophets (e.g., Amos) but also the so-called books of history (e.g., Judges). In those writings there are at least two promises for the future. The first is the promise of the monarchy and the second the promise of God's decisive act in history to right the wrongs of society.

The promise of the monarchy is given in the midst of Israel's efforts to make their new land a place free of oppression. The Israelites were no match for the Philistines. For a time it appeared that they had traded oppression to the Egyptians for another oppression—military subjection to the Philistines. The Israelites were a loose confederation of tribes, bound together only by their allegiance to Yahweh. The Philistines were a united people, capable therefore of military aggression to which the Israelite tribes were ill-equipped to respond.

In that context of division and oppression the Israelites debated the promises and perils of the monarchy (e.g., Judges 9 and 1 Samuel 8). The adoption of a monarchy seemed to some that Israel was caving in to the desire to "be like all the nations" (1 Sam. 8:20). Implicit in the resistance to the monarchy was Israel's commitment to its distinctiveness among the other nations. Kings and all of the political structure they brought were associated in the experience of the Hebrews with oppression and injustice. Some among them feared the royal consciousness that was sure to come with the monarchy, and they rightly feared that the royal consciousness would suffocate their unique consciousness as a distinctive people of God. God alone was to rule over them, and no human king could replace that rule. But practical considerations prevailed. There was no other way to achieve a united front against the Philistines and to sustain existence against the oppression of the enemy. Another liberation wrought by the hand of God was needed.

So God promises a king "for myself" (1 Sam. 16:1) and sends Samuel to anoint David. Putting aside all of the historical and literary problems connected with the rise of the monarch, one point emerges: The institution of the monarchy was God's act to empower Israel against the Philistines. The monarchy was the means by which God could once again liberate the people from the oppressive power of another nation. To be sure, the anointing of a king set in motion a struggle to understand and execute the monarchy as God intended it. One might argue that the people of Israel never prevailed in that struggle, and human sin thwarted the divine plan. In theory the king was to be God's servant, answerable to God—a constitutional monarchy of sorts. But kings, the great and legendary David included, persisted in the abuse of the power.

That struggle notwithstanding, the monarchy is another instance of God's effort to secure freedom for Israel—a life free of oppression and humiliation at the hands of excessive power. The promise of a

Davidic dynasty partakes of the same character (2 Sam. 7:11b-17; 23:5). The people could not live in security so long as the succession to the monarchy was left in the hands of charismatic leaders. The experience of the judges taught Israel that lesson. Security necessitated clear lines of succession—a dynasty. So, the promise to David further explicates God's concern for the lives of the people.

The divine institution of Israel's monarchy and the Davidic dynasty suggest the political interests of social ministry. Given the political realities of life, there must be ordered governance if life is to be lived free of tyranny and chaos. A people's land cannot be satisfactory without orderliness. The church is never able, therefore, to dissociate itself from the political realm. The Old Testament stories give us clues as to the nature and purpose of our political involvement. Its goal is always to see God's will for freedom and order realized. The political ministry of the church is necessitated by the quality of the divine care for this realm of life. The church then becomes a guardian of political power, attempting to insure that people are not oppressed by abusive power or by social chaos.

But the promise of the monarchy has still another aspect: the promise of a king faithful to God. This motif of promise is set in motion by God's rejection of Saul and the anointing of David (1 Samuel 16) and is continued in the prophets of the ninth century (e.g., 1 Kings 19:15-18). But the motif is found most clearly in the classical prophets of later centuries, where there is a recurring promise of a new king who would rule with justice and faithfulness.

The relevant passages are Isa. 9:2-7; 11:1-5; Mic. 5:2-4; Jer. 23:1-8 (cf. 33:14-16); and Zech. 9:9-10. These so-called messianic passages are prophetic anticipations of the advent of a king who would fulfill the obligations of the office with faithfulness to God. They are the promise of God spoken through the prophet that the political leadership of the nation would not be abandoned to human failures. These passages present a number of the characteristics of the future, ideal king. The king will possess wisdom and understanding (Isa. 11:2) and have a relationship of faithfulness with God (Isa. 11:5; Mic. 5:4). He will break the grip of oppression (Isa. 9:4), bring peace (Isa. 9:7; Jer. 23:6; Micah 5:4; Zech. 9:10), and rule with righteousness and justice (Isa. 9:7; 11:4; Jer. 23:5). The anticipation of the fulfillment of the promise expressed in these passages is also evident in the enthronement of the king depicted in the royal Psalms (e.g., 2, 18, 20, 21, 45, 72, 89, 110, and 132). Many of these same features of the future king expressed in the messianic passages are implied in

Messianic Hope

those psalms.[4] In the context of the anticipation and the series of disappointments with royal figures, the "messianic hope" took root— the hope for a figure in the distant future who would be God's true anointed.

The prophetic literature witnesses the way in which the promise of God is connected with political leaders. This promise never reached fulfillment in the way it was understood. But the promise of sound political rule is central to what God desires for people. That point alone should keep the church aware of its responsibility to nurture and support effective political leadership—leadership that insures justice and equity in our society. While in our pluralistic society a political system such as Israel's is unworkable, still the necessity of political leadership committed to the cause of social justice is mandated by the story of Israel and the monarchy.

The second major motif of promise in the prophetic literature is for the decisive act of God to right the wrongs of society. That promise is never separated from the pledge of a faithful king, for God's righting of society's wrongs most often requires a monarch who serves as God's instrument to accomplish that goal. But the images of that important day include noteworthy features. This hope is founded on the prophetic concept of the "day of the Lord" (*yom yahweh*), God's decisive victory over the forces of opposition (e.g., Amos 5:18-20).[5] God's victory over injustice and oppression is conceived of as a worldly event. That is, these are images of what will take place in this time and space frame we know as historical reality. They are not to be confused with the later images of an apocalyptic restoration—an event that lies beyond the boundaries of history.

Among the most important images of that future day are Isa. 2:1-4; (cf. Mic. 4:1-4); 11:6-9; 54:13-14; 55:12-13; 56:6-8; and Jer. 31:31-34. A composite of the features of that time of divine victory produces the following: The law will be central to society (Isa. 2:3) and obeyed out of the inner lives of people (Jer. 31:33); God (or the righteous king) will judge with justice and equity (Isa. 2:4), and righteousness will reign (Isa. 54:14); it will be a time of peace (*shalom*) among humans (Isa. 2:4; 55:12) and between humans and the natural order (Isa. 11:6-9; 55:12-13); war, oppression, and fear will not exist (Isa. 54:14), and the "knowledge" of God will prevail among all (Isa. 11:9; 54:13; Jer. 31:34); prosperity and plenty will exist (Isa. 54:11-13) within an inclusive society (Isa. 56:6-8).

Within these images of the future dwells the mandate of the ministry of the church. It is to seek a society in which the divine

Goals of the Church

intent of the law is lived, where peace and harmony prevail, where justice and inclusivism are common, where society and nature live at peace, and where all enjoy the benefits of prosperity. The ministry of the church to society finds in such images as these the goals for its work—however difficult and sometimes unlikely their attainment may be. Through the prophets God has promised just such a day as described here, and it behooves the church to become co-workers with God in the realization of that vision of the future.

That vision of God's decisive victory over the opposing forces is expressed in one other prophetic genre. As the hope for that decisive victory was conceived in greater and greater symbolism, it took on an otherworldly quality and was thought of less a historical event than one that transcended the scope of history. The hope gave rise to that literature which we call apocalyptic.[6] In the Old Testament the apocalyptic hope is best represented in the last six chapters of Daniel.[7] As read

These chapters are believed to have been written during a time when the Jewish people were suffering under the oppressive rule of the Seleucid king, Antiochus Epiphanes IV, ca. 165 B.C.E. He attempted to unify his kingdom under one religion, law, and custom, which for Jews meant the suppression of the Sabbath, circumcision, and dietary laws. Those who refused to obey were punished with death. He scandalized the Jewish people with an altar to Zeus, erected in the temple ("the abomination that makes desolate," Dan. 11:31). Amid those circumstances the author of Daniel described in poetic symbolism God's conquest over such alien forces. Against the beasts of foreign powers there comes "one like a human being" to whom is given everlasting dominion (Dan. 7:13). God's conquest of the oppressive forces of evil are sure for those blessed "who persevere" (Dan. 12:12).

The apocalyptic language of Daniel, however enigmatic, articulates a general theme, specifically, the assurance that God will not allow the political forces of evil to prevail but shall bring a victory for the faithful. It is a message of the good news of hope for a desperate, despairing people who are threatened with death for obeying their religious law. The Book of Daniel shines a beam of promise into the darkness of persecution; it announces release from oppression and pledges freedom. The force that overcomes the evil of Antiochus is none other than divine. But that promise stirred hope and determination to withstand whatever the oppressor offered. Not accidentally the Jewish revolt led by Judas Maccabees against Antiochus and his forces occurred nearly contemporaneously with the time we believe the author of Daniel to have written his stirring message. The author, it seems, evoked not passive waiting for God's action, but determined action in the name of God.

God's promise expressed in apocalyptic imagery is one of freedom and dignity in the face of overwhelming opposition. That message calls the church to be diligent in announcing just such promise for all those oppressed and mired in despair. Not a hope that "lets God do it," but one that empowers the human spirit with the divine endorsement. The ministry of the church in society is committed to that kind of message of empowerment, enabling the weak and mustering courage among the exploited.

Summary

What is remarkable in this brief survey of the promises of God in the Old Testament is the way in which divine care for the total life of humanity is once again expressed, even as we witnessed it in the images of God in the same body of literature (see chap. 1 above). God promises life conditions that we would describe as physical, and worldly, not just spiritual: land, descendants, political justice, prosperity, peace, and freedom from oppression, to name just a few. Two familiar messages for the church emerge from all of this. First, our God is committed to the total well-being of humanity and, second, that commitment is expressed in a resolve to alter the nature of human life in its totality.

The promise-fulfillment theme in the Old Testament is not irrelevant to social ministry. On the contrary, the persistent theme of promise is one that becomes the core of the church's efforts to serve society. In the formula, "behold, the days are coming," the church finds its commission for this very day. Far from nurturing passivity in the face of oppression, want, and injustice, the biblical images of the future stir commitment to God's commitments, actions to anticipate God's act, and determination to match the divine resolve. When we turn to the New Testament and its visions of the future, the same results emerge.

The Future in the New Testament

The overspill of promise, so characteristic of Israel's history, is also witnessed in the New Testament. The early Christians believed that in Christ God was fulfilling the promise to Israel. Jesus was, they asserted, the Messiah—the anointed one promised by the prophets (cf., Luke 24:27; Acts 8:26-35). Matthew goes to great lengths to structure the entire story of Jesus around the fulfillment of Old Testament prophecy (e.g., Matt. 2:5-6). The bold and almost incredible claim was that the anticipation of the ideal king found its fruition in Jesus of Nazareth (e.g., Matt. 21:4-5).

But the fulfillment of the promise spilled over into a new promise. God's work in history was not completed with the advent of Christ. There would be another advent—a reappearing of Christ in glory. So, the early Christians looked back to Jesus' historical ministry, death, and resurrection, but they also looked forward to a future time when the full meaning of that past event would be realized. The promise of the future arises, the early Christians claimed, from Jesus' own proclamation. According to the Gospels, Jesus spoke of a future coming of the kingdom of God in its fullness (e.g., Mark 13 and its parallels), and of the appearance of the "Son of Man" in glory (e.g., Mark 8:38). The Jesus of the Gospels consequently speaks of God's reign as both a present reality (e.g., Matt. 12:28) and as a promise of a future event (e.g., Matt. 8:11). Writers of the New Testament documents developed the future hope of Christ's reappearance on the basis of the tradition of Jesus' words on the subject.

The New Testament literature is, therefore, filled with the promise of the Parousia (the appearance of the glorified Christ). Using the image of the arrival of the monarch in one of the villages of the realm, the first Christians pictured the arrival of their sovereign. With the parousia the conditions of human life would be radically transformed into what God had desired for people from the very beginning. The image of that "end time" concerns us. What is it that God promises to do for humans when the divine kingdom is brought to its full realization? The images of that event are found scattered throughout the pages of the New Testament, but two of the most prominent ones are those offered by the apostle Paul and by John, the seer of Patmos.

The Future in Paul

Of Paul's several passages concerned with the promise of the final, decisive act of God (e.g., 1 Thess. 4:15-18) one in particular stands out, namely, 1 Corinthians 15. In this chapter Paul is responding to doubt about the promise of the believers' resurrection. Apparently there were among the Christians of the church at Corinth those who found such a promise incredible. Paul argues at some length for the resurrection of Christian believers at the end time (vs. 1-19). Then he sketches the conditions brought about by the reappearance of Christ (vs. 20-28). He proposes that the raising of Christ was the "first fruits" of a general resurrection. With that raising of the Christians comes "the end" (*telos*, "the goal") God seeks, "when [Christ] hands over the kingdom to God the Father" (v. 24).

The goal of God's work in Christ is achieved, however, only after Christ has destroyed "every ruler (*archēn*) and every authority (*exousian*) and power (*dynamin*)," (v. 24). Finally, "the death" (*ho thanatos*) is abolished (v. 26). Each of these is called an "enemy" (*echthros*, v. 25). The opponents of God are rule, authority, power, and death, in Paul's view.

Walter Wink has persuasively demonstrated that these are among the terms of power the New Testament uses "to mean both heavenly and earthly, divine and human good and evil powers." As forces of evil, opposed to God, they represent both the outward, historical and the inward, spiritual realities that frustrate the divine purpose. They cannot be entirely spiritualized, therefore, into cosmic entities beyond the scope of history. Rather, they are historical entities that in their inward nature share a spiritual reality. First Cor. 2:8, for instance, suggests the ambiguous way in which these terms are used, referring at once to both historical and cosmic phenomena.[8]

What Paul visualizes in passages such as 1 Cor. 15:24-26 is the defeat of all those "enemies" of God in both their cosmic and historical reality. It is not a vision of the overcoming of only transhuman powers that reside in the cosmos beyond the reach of humans. It is the defeat of both those cosmic, spiritual forces, as well as their manifestation in historical reality. Paul is speaking, for instance, of the abolishment of those "rules" that perpetuate the cycle of poverty in the world in addition to psychological, social, and spiritual forces that contribute to such a cycle.

The church cannot, then, view this final victory of God as one that has no concrete reference to the conditions of society today. Our contention is that these images of the final victory of God suggest the nature of our ministries in society in the present—that what God promises to abolish in the end time is what we must be working to abolish in the present time. Moreover, when we work to oppose concrete, historical manifestations of the enemies of God, we also work at the dismantling of the spiritual, cosmic sources of enmity. If that principle is sound, Paul's image of God's final goal for humanity becomes our immediate goal. Our ministries are directed to all the historical sources of those powers that deter the fulfillment of God's plan. Paul especially enables us to see how those forces become embedded in institutionalized forms in our world—in rules, authorities, and powers. For instance, he helps us understand that racism has become institutionalized within the structures of our society. The defeat of those forces is our goal no less than it is God's goal for human existence.

The Future in Revelation

The image of the future expressed by Paul is often, if not always, apocalyptic.[9] But in the Book of Revelation we find a fully apocalyptized image of the promise of God for the future. That is, the form of the hope expressed in Revelation most clearly has the two chief distinctive features of the apocalyptic genre. First, it visualizes the conquest of God as an event that lies on and/or beyond the borders of time and history. The fulfillment of God is in a "new heaven and a new earth" (21:1). Second, it articulates the promise and the struggle for its fulfillment in elaborate imagery (e.g., the "beasts" of chap. 13). Typical of apocalyptic imagery is an abundance of animal and numerical symbols. The imagery is so pervasive that it seems almost a "code" for the interpreter to crack.

The Revelation of John shares much with the Book of Daniel, discussed above.[10] It was apparently written to a number of Christian communities in Asia Minor during or just prior to a time of persecution at the hands of the Romans (ca. 95 C.E.). Most often scholars argue that the present form of the book addressed a situation in which Christians are being threatened with death for their faith, during a time when the Roman emperor cult was being advanced in this region and with it the demand that the divinity of Caesar be confessed. It is possible that even John's own exile to Patmos (Rev. 1:9) was a result of this situation.[11]

In that context John wrote a message of hope and encouragement in which he used established apocalyptic images to portray the victory of God over the forces oppressing the Christian communities. In lucid terms he identified Rome and the emperor cult with satanic evil (e.g., chap. 13) and described God's victory over that evil (e.g., chap. 20). As is the case in Paul's images of the future, John pictured the historical reality of Roman arrogance and abuse of power as an expression of the cosmic reality of evil. Our concern, however, must be limited to the conditions brought about by God's defeat of those forces.

The most striking image of the transformation of the human condition is found in Revelation 21 and 22. There John describes "a new heaven and a new earth" that replaces the present ones. Among their characteristics are the absence of death, mourning, crying, and pain (21:4). The fullness of God's dwelling with humans is the alleviation of all the causes and expressions of hurt. In 22:3 the vision includes the summary that "nothing accursed (*katathema*) will be found there anymore." Because all of the causes of human suffering are "cursed" by God, they are all the objects of the final divine victory.

This image of the end time is often evoked as an assurance of the destiny of our loved ones after death. There is truth in that application of John's message. But equally relevant, this apocalyptic image of the future informs us of God's stubborn determination to alleviate human suffering in all of its forms—to strike at the very heart of that which inhibits full humanity. It informs us, yes, but it also motivates us to make God's enemies our enemies and the objects of our ministry. To overcome the power of death in human life, to annihilate the causes of mourning and tears, to dismantle the accursed is our mission now, because it is God's mission.

Still, the message of Revelation as it speaks to the ministry of the church in society is more. First, God's victory as it is portrayed in Revelation is the liberation of an oppressed people. The first readers of the book were being denied their freedom by the oppressive demands of the state. John's message is that once again God sides with the victims of oppression and promises to aid and vindicate them— the same message we found rooted in the exodus story (see chap. 1 above).

Second, Revelation points to the potential evil of a political system. Revelation is a very political book. It lashes out in absolute terms against political systems that dehumanize people and declares that the power of evil comes to expression in such political systems. John announces, therefore, that there are limits to political power. A political system becomes satanic when it seeks to suppress freedom and touts itself as the ultimate authority in human life. Significantly, for John a political system can become an idol, when secular power is deified. The warning for us is that government does not always function as God's instrument for proper order (cf. Romans 13; 1 Pet. 2:13-15). Paul and the author of 1 Peter each point out the sense in which governmental order is a means by which God protects order and justice in a land and holds the power of human sin in check. In that function the Christian is called to cooperate with the political system. But government is liable to corruption and distortion. John of Patmos issues the call to oppose political systems that have failed to function as God intended and have become instruments of that which opposes the divine will.

John of Patmos mandates a watchfulness with regard to political power and its assertions over human life. By implication, therefore, the Book of Revelation teaches the necessity of political involvement as the means by which Christians guard against political abuse. Moreover, Revelation is realistic about the seductive power of political systems. John recognizes the attractiveness of the peace, security, and relative prosperity brought by Roman rule (cf. 18:1-19).

③ Third, the image of God in Revelation is clearly that of one who shares the suffering of the innocent. At this point John's image of God coincides with what we found in both the Old and New Testaments (see chaps. 1 and 2 above). The God of Revelation is not the triumphal deity removed from the pain of the divine family, but rather one who is moved to act triumphantly precisely because of the divine identification with humans. This point is clearly implied in several ways in the Revelation of John, not least of all in the image of the "lamb." This image is used of Christ no less than twenty-nine times. It represents the death of Christ (e.g., 5:12) and his lordship as a result of that death (e.g., 17:14). In Christ God has shared the suffering and death of oppressive political and religious regimes, since Christ's death was at the hands of just such a regime.

④ Fourth, Revelation suggests again (as does Paul) how evil becomes expressed in specific realities. The defeat of evil is not only the defeat of some supra-human, cosmic figures but the conquest of concrete historical embodiments of evil. Revelation does not describe evil in terms of spiritual forces that are defeated only by God's work. The Roman government and its representatives in Asia Minor are forms of that evil to be dealt with by the Christians in their immediate present.

Therefore, and finally, Revelation implies that humans share responsibility for the defeat of evil. To be sure, the book stresses the role of the divine action in overcoming evil. But at the same time it implies a human responsibility for that conquest. If God is aligned against evil, the people of God are likewise sided against evil. Christians are by implication God's co-workers against even the mighty power of the Roman usurpation of divine prerogative. Revelation does not sanction a passive waiting for God's act, but a faithful action with God to oppose the opponents of the divine.

Interestingly, the image of the liberating, passionate, and active God of Revelation brings us full circle to where the discussion began, namely, with the image of God in the exodus story. The image of God is consistent, but so too are the images of the divine historical and eschatological work.

Conclusion

The visions of the future articulated in the New Testament, like the ones in the Old Testament, are images that evoke and motivate human agency on behalf of God's plan for the future. The images of what God will finally bring into reality in the last days of history concern what needs to be attempted in the here and now. God's promises of a new future are invitations into that future. They are gestures of welcome into a life that shares the features of the future that God has promised. As such these images are empowering symbols of what is possible, even amid situations that make them seem most impossible. If, for instance, the possibility of Christian resistance against the might of Rome seemed incredible, the message of John of Patmos was intended to facilitate a birth of courage in the Christians to join God's battle against the enemies of the divine will.

Far from finding these images irrelevant, our social ministry finds both its goals and motivation there. Through them we know what God wants and to what God is committed. Consequently, through them we find ourselves empowered to seek the divine *telos* (goal) of human life. Our ministry is mandated in the promise of God's ministry in history.

The Bible clearly articulates the mandate for and the call to social ministry, but does it provide any specific direction for that ministry? That topic is addressed in Part Two.

Notes

1. Moltmann, *The Theology of Hope*, 106.
2. Cf. Kysar, *Proclamation*, 28–30.
3. Brueggemann, *The Land*.
4. Cf. McCurley and Reumann, *Witness of the Word*, chaps. 21 and 22.

5. Cf. von Rad, *Theology of the Old Testament* 2:119–25.

6. Among the literature on Old Testament apocalyptic cf. Hanson, *The Dawn of Apocalyptic*; and Hanson, ed., *Visionaries and Their Apocalypses*, as well as Russell, *Jewish Apocalyptic* and *Apocalyptic Ancient and Modern*.

7. Among the commentaries on Daniel cf. Towner, *Daniel*, and Porteous, *Daniel*.

8. Wink, *Naming the Powers*, 100.

9. For the argument that Paul's theology is thoroughly apocalyptic cf. Beker, *Paul the Apostle*, *Paul's Apocalyptic Gospel*, and *The Triumph of God*.

10. For the Jewish setting of Christian apocalypticism cf. Collins, *The Apocalyptic Imagination*.

11. Among the commentaries on Revelation which prove most helpful are these: Caird, *St. John the Divine*; Mounce, *The Book of Revelation*; Charles, *The Revelation of St. John*; and Krodel, *Revelation*. Cf. Schüssler Fiorenza, *The Book of Revelation* and Collins, *Crisis and Catharsis*. Fiorenza and Collins help us see in the apocalyptic genre a medium for nurturing social resistance to oppression.

PART TWO

*Practical
Directions for
Social Ministry*

5

Changing the
Popular
Consciousness

The first movement of the grand symphony we have been attending was comprised of the biblical roots for social ministry itself, roots that are found in at least four dimensions of the biblical witness. They all provide the foundations for the mission of the church in contemporary society and comprise the identity of the Christian people as ministers to society. From the theoretical foundations of social ministry, we now move on to seek the practical directions for social ministry in the Bible.

The scope of the subject cannot be completely summarized here.[1] Those practical issues that are most important and find their resolution in the biblical faith have arisen out of efforts to enable congregations to strengthen their social ministries. They are herein structured as a movement from broadest (the consciousness of persons in contemporary American society) to narrowest (the specific concerns usually raised within a congregation).

The thesis of this chapter is that the church needs to effect a transformation of popular consciousness if its social ministry is to be vigorous. The immediate task before us calls for two things. The first is to argue that there is a need for a fundamental transformation of contemporary American consciousness, if the church's ministry to society is to be successful. The second is to suggest the way in which the biblical witness aids in practical efforts to effect that transformation.

The Need for a New Consciousness

The ministry of the church to society is seriously impaired today by a general mentality or consciousness in America, a set of presuppositions about reality and self that shape perception and orient behavior. The consciousness referred to here has to do with the often unconscious and uncritical acceptance of a certain perspective that determines self-identity and purpose. It can also be referred to, for example, as a mentality, worldview, or paradigm.

An anecdote will help illustrate what is meant by this consciousness. When I was a very young child, I somehow came to believe that everything that was real was for me and me alone. Therefore, the playground did not exist until I decided to go to there. It came into existence by the power of my will, and it passed from existence as soon as I left it. This radical egotism was my way of viewing the whole of reality. Fortunately, I soon came to realize that this view of things was erroneous and that I played a much smaller role in the total scheme of things. The point is that my childhood view of reality was an unrecognized consciousness that determined the way I lived (however unfortunate that was). I did not intentionally choose the thought process but discovered that I did indeed view reality in that way. It shaped my entire perception of reality and determined the way I acted in relationship to other people and things.

Society for the most part shapes within us a consciousness of the way things are. That mentality is in the air we breathe from our first breath and is nurtured by all of our experiences in life, because those experiences occur within society. It is self-authenticating in that it determines the way we experience reality, which in turn authenticates our reality. Our consciousness is seldom clear to us and rarely abstracted for scrutiny; rather, it is presupposed, infrequently raised for critical appraisal, and rarely challenged.[2]

The pervasive consciousness of most contemporary American Christians is one that generally makes it difficult for them to comprehend and respond to a call to social justice. For instance, an absence of a consciousness of social solidarity renders impotent the call for action on poverty. Because we do not have a strong sense of the interdependence of human life in our society, it is difficult for us to understand the importance of effecting significant change in the social, political, and economic conditions of others.

A presupposition in this chapter is that one of the reasons our ministries to social needs are weakened is that we have not examined and altered the fundamental consciousness of our society and more specifically of our congregations. This is due to the fact that the church itself embraces that societal consciousness and is hesitant to address it in a critical manner. Moreover, it is difficult to know how to go about the task of altering such a fundamental phenomenon as a cultural consciousness. Indeed, some would argue that it is impossible to do so. The church would hardly seem equipped to undertake such a monumental task. But as long as we fail to do so, our efforts to nurture a commitment to ministry to society seem doomed, since social values play only a minimal role at best in the popular mentality of contemporary Americans.

An example is close at hand. Throughout recent decades the church has attempted to address the problem of racial discrimination in society. In the past several years, however, we have become aware that the strides we thought we had made toward racial equality in America are not as significant as we might have once supposed. What has surfaced again and again in many parts of the country is evidence that the fundamental change of attitude and presuppositions about persons of different races has not been significantly altered. It appears that the essential consciousness of people is still not able to accommodate a basic social equality.

The problem is fundamentally one of perception. It is well articulated in a study published under the title *Habits of the Heart*. The researchers sought to discover the basic consciousness of white, middle-class Americans living in geographically diverse parts of the nation. They sought to learn through interviews "what resources Americans have for making sense of their lives, how they think about themselves and their society, and how their ideas relate to their actions."[3] What the team of interviewers found was sobering. The ultimate goals for life, according to those interviewed, were success, understood primarily in terms of economic progress; freedom, understood primarily in terms of "being left alone" (that is, free from constraint); and justice, understood primarily as opportunity to pursue whatever an individual construes to be happiness. The mentality of those interviewed reflected a radical individualism that stressed the supreme importance of self-reliance, of "making something of yourself." Their lives were structured around an extreme privatism. The community that was sought most often took the form of "life-style enclaves" —exclusivistic groupings of persons with similar interests and that celebrate a "narcissism of similarity."

Public life is dominated by self-interest. It is difficult, the researchers observe, for us to "conceive of a common good or a public interest that recognizes economic, social, and cultural differences among people but see them all as parts of a single society on which they all depend."[4] Citizenship beyond one's own local community is difficult. Even the church tends to be viewed as an extension of the family or an enlarged "life-style enclave." Consequently a vagueness about the concept of the public good pervades our thought, making it difficult to conceive a social vision that fulfills the good of all.

The researchers were forced to the conclusion that ours is a culture of fragmentation, one in which there is no sense of a overall pattern to life. A reconstitution of the social world is demanded, the writers concluded, if our society is to remain viable. Yet the conclusions are not totally pessimistic. The authors suggest that few Americans are satisfied with their lives, particularly with a way of life that attaches highest value to personal success and consumerism. There is a disillusionment with the results such a way of life brings.

> If there are vast numbers of a selfish, narcissistic "me generation" in America, we did not find them, but we certainly did find that the language of individualism, the primary American language of self-understanding, limits the ways in which people think. . . . Many Americans are concerned to find meaning in life not primarily through self-cultivation but through intense relations with others.[5]

The problem seems to be that the resources for finding such a connectedness with others are not present in the common American mentality.

Toward a New Consciousness

The need, therefore, is to transform that basic consciousness so diffuse in contemporary American culture. Can we define the directions such a transformation might take? What kind of changes are called for that would produce a mentality more conducive to social welfare? If the church should undertake a transformation of this cultural consciousness, what are the characteristics of the new consciousness it might seek? A number of features of the change we must seek can be isolated for consideration.

From Spiritual to Holistic

The first is a transformation from a spiritual to holistic consciousness. We are captivated by the spiritual, internal life of the individual to the point that the whole life situation of people is deemphasized. This spiritualization of life takes at least two forms in our society today.

In its secular form spiritualization is the idolizing of the internal, emotional, psychological state of a person.[6] In this form it nurtures the view that nothing matters so long as the individual is "well-adjusted," that is, internally content with her or his situation. The idol of emotional well-being results in the tolerance of injustice and suffering by means of the assumption that, whatever the conditions in which people live, all that matters is their emotional contentment. For instance, the unjust treatment of women in our society is dismissed with the fact (and it is a fact) that many women are absolutely content with their role as submissive homemakers. On the basis of that fact, such women disregard the question of the opportunities for other kinds of fulfilment in our society. Or the poor are often said to be "happy" in their poverty; it has taught them patience and contentment with their lot. Such a view (with its limited truths) becomes a rationale for the injustice of poverty and an excuse for passivity in the face of the disproportionate distribution of wealth.

But the religious form of spiritualism concerns us even more. It takes the shape of the view that one's private relationship with God is all that matters. The "salvation of the soul" regardless of the state of the body is of utmost importance. The spiritualization of the biblical message in large part has allowed Christians to hold and sustain this view. The spiritual consciousness has altered the way in which the biblical message is heard and the way the gospel is experienced so as to authenticate the spiritualism. Christian spiritualism becomes therefore an incentive to ignore the social, political, economic conditions of people and to focus exclusively on their spiritual welfare. Seldom does one hear the church overtly endorse such a view as "let them starve but save their souls." But in more subtle ways the idolizing of the spiritual diminishes our commitment to ministry to society.

That this view is solidly embedded in popular Christian mentality struck me in the process of doing Bible studies with lay people. Jesus' beatitude about the poor is known only in its Matthean form ("Blessed are the poor in spirit," Matt. 5:3) and rarely in its Lukan form ("Blessed are you who are poor," Luke 6:20). Biblical passages having to do with God's desire to change the physical conditions of people are transmuted into statements of the divine intent to change spiritual conditions. For instance, Jesus' sermon in the synagogue at Nazareth speaks of his being sent to "proclaim release to the captives and recovery of sight to the blind, to let the oppressed go free" (Luke 4:18). Those words are most often thoroughly spiritualized. The captives are those imprisoned by personal sin; the blind are those who do not know the gospel; and the oppressed those held back by guilt. On one occasion, when I protested this kind of interpretation of such a passage, one lay person said to me that her pastor had taught her to look for the spiritual meaning of the Bible as she read it.

The results of such a popular mentality is that social action, ministry to the material needs of people, is put in subordination to spiritual concerns. The consciousness expressed in such a spiritualizing of the biblical message is one that assumes the greatest worth is found in the intangible, internal life of a person and that her or his outward conditions matter less.

Tangible
Doctor

What is called for is a transformation from this narrow spiritualism into a holism. The preoccupation with the spiritual can be overcome only by a concern for the whole of human existence. What we really need involves a rethinking of what is meant in the first place by the concept of the spiritual in the context of Christian faith and life. The spiritual dimension of life needs to be reconceived as the quality of relationships within the total human situation—physical, economic, social, as well as religious. Spirituality might well be thought of in terms of the way it is inclusive of the other material dimensions of human existence—in other words, in holistic terms. What modern medicine has discovered and is teaching is the consummate relatedness of all dimensions of human life, so that, for instance, the states of mind and the body affect each other. We need to rediscover and teach the way in which the so-called spiritual condition of persons is inseparable from their material conditions. Only then can we muster a ministry that addresses the whole person.

As John Howard Yoder has counseled, it is necessary for us to avoid two extremes in our attitude toward society and particularly the social structures within which we live. On the one hand is what might be called the "pietistic" extreme that assumes that Christianity has to do with personal and not social ethics. On the other hand there is a common position that might be characterized as "ascetic." It regards social structures as evil, impure, and defiling, counseling that the Christian avoid them at all risk.[7]

The holistic ministry of the church assumes that the social structures within which people live are not necessarily evil and that they are no less important than the personal, spiritual welfare of the individuals within them. Hence it cannot elevate only one dimension of the message of the gospel, nor say that the good news of God's act in Christ has impact only on one's relationship with God. But it teaches that God's decisive act was for the salvation of the total human condition. We will achieve such a holistic view only as we alter that popular contemporary American mentality that divides the whole and orders the parts in terms of some set of priorities.

From Individual to Corporate

The second feature of the new consciousness we must seek in American culture involves a change of consciousness from individual to corporate. The research summarized in *Habits of the Heart* makes clear that we are imprisoned in a radical individualism that effectively isolates us from one another. Such an individualism has deep roots in American history and self-understanding, as the researchers show. Indeed, in some ways the individualism of Americans made the founding and development of our nation possible. But the degree of individualistic self-understanding has gradually increased, until today we experience more of its detriments than its benefits.

The painful results of the current radical individualism include the tremendous loneliness experienced by many of us and the desperate search for community that makes possible the extremes seen in the rise of cults in our society. We seem to be starving for community, suffocating in our privatistic isolation from others. The expressed need for community is, however, being fulfilled in forms of pseudo-community most often through the medium of television. The isolation seems overcome without risk to individual integrity by the identification with those single-dimensional characters who enter our homes through electronic means. Hence, thousands try to find community in being part of the families portrayed in situation comedies, the relationships among characters in a soap opera, or even the team of reporters on the evening news.

In place of such pseudo-community a new corporate consciousness needs to arise to cure our isolation and provide the life-sustaining air of genuine community. We need a transformation of how we understand ourselves, as well as a mutation of our concept of relatedness with others. For the corporatism that must replace our radical individualism roots in a sense of being not primarily individuals but parts of a communal whole. We tend to define ourselves, first of all, as separate, distinct entities, whose lives are independent of other humans and all forms of living beings. We start in other words with the isolated individual self as fundamental reality. Then, on the basis of that independent self, we try to conceive of our relationship with other humans and with nature as a whole. The transformation I have in mind calls for the reversal of the order of that process. We are first of all creatures within a context of relatedness. Our embryonic conception is the result of an interrelatedness and our maturation as individuals is always a social process. We are then secondarily individuals and primarily segments of a society.

To start with the social reality of human life and to move from there to a sense of individuality is logical, given what we know of human life today as a result of the social and biological sciences. Surely, social science has demonstrated to the satisfaction of most that there is no such thing as the isolated individual—that all human life is a reflection of the social realities within which that life exists. You and I must admit that we are who we are today because of social forces upon us, far more than because of independent personal decisions and actions (and even those decisions and actions are themselves in most cases expressions of our socialization, our social environment). Moreover, as we learn our social interrelatedness and begin to take it seriously, perhaps we can also learn a natural ecology as well. As a human community we are interrelated with the natural world around us in an inseverable interdependence.

If such a transformation from individualism to corporatism is possible, the ministry of the church to society becomes possible. With a new sense of corporate interrelatedness our bond with other humans as humans becomes not only clear but self-evident. If that were to become the case, the social admonitions of the church would no longer ask us to reach out of our pure isolation into the similarly isolated world of others. It would then be clear that our fate is tied up with the fate of others—their conditions are ours and ours theirs. This is not to say that social ministry arising from a consciousness of corporate relationship is founded purely on self-interest, although that point is not unimportant. What is different in the consciousness of corporality is that the relatedness is already there. You would not be asking me to establish a relationship with the poor in the ghetto of my city and then work on their behalf. That relationship would already exist for me, if my mentality of myself had transcended the radical individualism so typical of our society. With a consciousness of our interrelatedness the exhortation to be concerned for the other is received within a different context. Yes, my life is connected with the lives of the migrant farm workers; it only makes sense that with that connectedness I should be concerned for them.

The social ministry of the church rises or falls with the congregation's sense of corporality with all others and with nature itself.

From Powerless to Empowered

Third, the transformation of consciousness we seek is one from powerless to empowered. There is in American culture today an ever increasing sense of impotence to effect social change. This fear of powerlessness is not restricted to the congregation; it is a social phenomenon.

The mentality of powerlessness in contemporary American culture arises from a number of facts, some of which are listed here. First, our individualistic mentality yields a sense of impotence in connection with altering the life conditions of ourselves or other people. The fact that we conceive of ourselves as locked into an individualistic existence means by itself that we have no power to effect matters that alter situations—either our own or that of others—because we have no connection with others. As we transform individual into corporate consciousness, we already begin to overcome our sense of powerlessness.

Second, our sense of powerlessness has been enhanced by the complexities of social problems. While we have been lured into a pretense of sublime individualism, our world has been rapidly shrinking in around us, actually bringing individuals and groups closer together. With that change, issues have become more and more intertwined with one another. To address the issue of unemployment today, for instance, necessitates having to address world, not simply local or even national, economics. Consequently, every action has far-reaching implications, and every problem widespread causes. Each social issue is like a giant octopus with each of its tentacles wrapped securely around other problems. The result is that we feel intimidated by the scope of our social problems.

This complexity gives rise to the third reason for powerlessness—"experts." We have come to believe that only experts can solve problems. We look for expertise for every imaginable problem, from the question of which toothpaste we should use to lessen the likelihood of cavities to the issue of how we achieve world peace. We have felt forced to abdicate our responsibility to the experts of the world and thereby to acknowledge our own powerlessness to act to resolve a problem. For instance, ordinary Americans seem to feel that they have little power to effect change in the way in which the needs of the poor are met in our society. That issue must be handled by those with the expertise to assess what constitutes poverty, what causes it, and how it can be overcome. On the other hand, the desperation of some inner-city neighborhoods to do something about the problem of drug abuse has empowered them to act. They have despaired over the power of governmental programs and police action to change their situation, as well as other experts in the field, so they have marshalled their own resources, in some cases with remarkable results.

The mentality of powerlessness must be replaced with a consciousness of empowerment. This means that we need to begin to think of ourselves as members of a body that does have resources for making significant changes. Again, if a corporality takes over the radical individualism that has grown like a cancer among us, empowerment is more likely to emerge. Empowerment means that people make the difference. It is a reaffirmation of the democratic principle that the power lies not with elected leaders or with experts but with the masses. Perhaps our own revolution lies too far in the distant past for us to grasp the potency of the people. It is the rebirth of that principle that lies at the heart of the need for a transformation from powerlessness to empowerment.

For Christians the social consciousness of powerlessness makes it difficult to appropriate the empowerment we believe is available in Christ. If we are sometimes frustrated by the way in which the divine promise of power for ministry falls on deaf ears in the congregation, might it not be because the current cultural mentality has so convinced people that they are powerless that any promise of empowerment seems like so much wishful thinking? The context of a new cultural consciousness will make it possible for people to hear and appropriate the promise of the divine empowerment for ministry.

From Charity to Justice

Fourth, our way of thinking and perceiving needs to move from charity to justice. In an even more direct way this mutation addresses social change. Contemporary American culture has found its identity in a sense of charity as the adequate response to human need. Charity is a limitation that cripples the ability of Americans to act for human welfare. Justice is the only adequate mentality.

By charity I mean that stance that assumes that I can adequately aid another in need by maintaining my own status, while condescending to assist the needy. It assumes a chasm between me and the needy other. It further assumes that chasm can be kept in place while I serve the other. Charity is the sharing of my excess for the sake of another who has too little, while at the same time assuring my continued excess. Charity of this kind is best known in economic matters but is not limited to that sphere. Perhaps the best example is charity as regards the issue of freedom. The assumption is that if my own freedom is vast enough and is not threatened, I can grant a degree of freedom to another. But it must be the case, dictates the mentality of charity, that my own freedom is not diminished by the freedom I grant to the other. So we men are willing to offer freedom of opportunity in the workplace to women only so long as it does not infringe upon our own unlimited freedom. When it does, charity has reached its limits. Resistance to quotas in hiring and promotion expressed in charges of "reverse discrimination" exemplify the limits of charity in matters having to do with both gender and racial issues.

Justice, on the other hand, begins with a different premise, namely, with a sense of solidarity with the condition of the other person and further assumes that service is rendered not from a distance but in relationship with the other. Justice seeks not the sharing of surplus on the part of a few with the many but the total redistribution of all the resources of a society. It presupposes restructuring social systems rather than the maintenance of the status quo. So, to use the illustration cited above, the liberation of women in our society calls for a full reordering of society and not a simple surrendering of some of the excess power vested in men. Justice demands that a society work intentionally to overcome the injustice of the past in order to include women and racial minorities.

To seek justice instead of charity means to rebuild the total social system from the foundation up and not simply to remodel its entryway. The transformation imagined in this case is a more perceptive vision of what is needed to effect real social change.[8]

From Achieved to Intrinsic Worth

The fifth dimension of the transformation involves a movement from achieved worth to intrinsic worth. The common American mentality is deeply rooted in the assumption that one's worth is a direct reflection of what one has been able to accomplish. The current mentality is well known and is the basis of the American work ethic, the foundation of which is the presupposition that the degree of achievement in the workplace is an indicator of the degree of worthiness of the individual. Once again, this feature of the current mentality is possible in large part because of the radical individualism of our tradition. It assumes that we all start out from the same place and the most worthy among us run the farthest before dropping over.

The consciousness of achieved worth is to be credited with driving many to accomplish the seemingly impossible—the "only-in-America" success stories we all know so well. But many are beginning to realize that personal worth achieved through performance has had negative results far more destructive than its positive results are constructive. Many of those negative results are evident to us today. They include a drive to succeed that has killed many before their maturity. Achieved worth has made single-issue people out of many of us, especially men who have neglected all else in life in order to win their value in their professions. As a consequence, marriages, families, personal health, and many other aspects of life have suffered. The achieved worth mentality has nurtured even in the most successful persons a self-doubt and uncertainty that has put contentment out of reach.

The achieved worth mentality has fostered an attitude toward ourselves that has made neurotics out of many of us. But equally serious is the attitude toward others produced by such a view of human worth. It has meant that those who have not achieved, for whatever reason, should be viewed as of lower value than the "successful." Because of the achieved worth mentality in American culture, we are forced into a gradation of personal worth. So we view persons as being of varying degrees of worth dependent on their degree of achievement. Such a perspective allows for the disregard of the needs of some, since they are of lower worth. This is especially evident in America today. We have experienced a new wave of immigrants to our land. Many of them come from cultures in which the concept of achieved worth does not prevail, and so they do not automatically express the drive toward accomplishment we have come to value so highly. From the perspective of those indoctrinated with the lie of achieved worth, these people are "worthless." They are subhuman, not entitled to our care and concern.

In contrast our national legacy also has a tradition of "intrinsic worth," nourished by its religious heritage. Such a view of human worth assumes that all persons are worthy by virtue of being human and nothing more. This view does not necessitate the grading of worth because worth is given in birth, not earned in accomplishment. Such a view seemed intended by the preamble of our Constitution in its declaration, "All men are created equal and endowed with certain alienable rights." While the exclusivity of those words (both explicit and implicit) is not to be denied, the sentiment reaches beyond the confines of achieved worth to something approaching intrinsic worth. If such a view of human worth prevailed and if it were expanded to include all humans (e.g., females, unlanded persons, and persons of different races), there would be no question as to the value of human life. No debate would be necessary, for instance, as to how much of a city's funds should be directed toward the care of the "street people" or those afflicted with AIDS.

Such a transformation from achieved to intrinsic worth entails ramifications beyond the scope of our analysis. It must be asked to what degree our economic system depends on a mentality of achieved worth and what would happen if we were ever to abandon that view in favor of one of intrinsic worth. To effect this transformation would be to transform for better or for worse much of what we have come to think of as the "American way of life."

It hardly needs to be said that the social ministry of the church depends on the concept of a form of intrinsic worth rooted in the universal scope of God's love. To transform the achieved worth mentality into one of intrinsic worth is part of what it means to cultivate the Christian gospel in lives of people. Such a transformation would be an effort to practice in society the kind of spirit revealed in the ministry of Jesus. The practice of that ministry would be a daring experiment to live in an atmosphere of unconditional human worth.

From Enslavement to Liberation

Finally, we might summarize the impact of such a transformation as the shift from enslavement to liberation. I mean to suggest here in summary fashion that we have become enslaved to the contemporary American mentality in such a way that we cannot experience the freedom we so much prize in this land. We have become prisoners of our own spirituality, radical individualism, powerlessness, charity, and conditional worth. In contrast we seldom experience the freedom of wholeness, corporateness, empowerment, justice, and unconditional worth.

To be sure, any cultural consciousness is an enslavement of a kind. It enslaves us to a particular way of experiencing reality and understanding ourselves. Freedom from some form of cultural consciousness is no more possible than freedom from the digestive system. But there are some cultural mentalities that enhance freedom and some that inhibit it. I suggest that, ironically, American consciousness, in its present form, enslaves more than it frees. Most important for the Christian is the fact that our contemporary American consciousness has imprisoned us from our needy neighbor. It has denied us our freedom to be for the other in his or her need. Rather than being free to respond to human needs, we are isolated from others by our individualism, trapped by our preoccupation with the spiritual, immobilized by our sense of powerlessness, mired down in our satisfaction with charity, and captivated by achieved worth. Consequently we have been robbed of our heritage in Christ—the heritage to be a people for others, as Christ was a man for others.

The transformation of consciousness sketched in these pages promises a freedom for the other—a freedom to respond fully and effectively to the needs of other humans. Therefore, the need for transformation is far from "un-American" but is in fact thoroughly American insofar as it promises a precious dimension to the freedom our forebear sought in coming to these shores. Far more important, however, is the fact that the new consciousness outlined above comprises some of the fundamentals of the Christian life-style.

Biblical Directions for a New Consciousness

But is such a transformation of consciousness possible? Even more problematic is whether the church can play a significant role in such a transformation. I am not so naive to think that both questions can be answered in the affirmative without qualification. But in the spirit of a new consciousness I affirm that there is an empowerment at the disposal of the church which makes possible a gradual and at least partial movement toward the transformation herein described. One of the encouraging things about the report of the researchers in *Habits of the Heart* is that many Americans are searching for something different and better for their lives.

If it is the case that the current American consciousness can undergo transformation and if the church can play a role in that change, we must ask how and with what resources? I shall attempt to address the second question first by arguing that the Bible offers us a resource for the transformation of cultural consciousness. Then together we will begin exploring means by which the church might use that resource in commencing the process of changing the cultural mentality.

The Bible as a Resource

The apostle Paul speaks several times of the fact that the gospel message itself is a transforming power in the lives of persons. In 2 Cor. 5:16-17 he wrote: "From now on, therefore, we regard no one from a human point of view; even though we once knew Christ from a human point of view, we know him no longer in that way. So if anyone is in Christ, there is a new creation: everything old has passed away; see, everything has become new!" The "human point of view" represents a consciousness, a mentality that is limited in its scope by the presuppositions of the world and culture. Paul claims that his own experience in Christ has brought a transformation of that consciousness and that he has come to experience life in a different way. This way of experiencing is so radically distinct that Paul can speak of it as a "new creation." He exhorts the Christians in Rome to appropriate for themselves the transformation to a new consciousness when he writes, "Do not be conformed to this world, but be transformed by the renewing of your minds" (Rom. 12:2).

We begin with Paul because he glimpsed the truth that the act of God in Christ altered the basic way in which humans view themselves and their experience. The proclamation of the good news of Christ is in itself, then, a consciousness-transforming endeavor. It remains only for us to understand the way in which our view of ourselves and reality are altered by the reception of the gift of God's love in Christ. I propose Paul knew it was a transformation that was not limited only to our relationship with God but that it transfigured all of our relationships—those with ourselves, with others, and with our world, as well as with God.

Indeed the entire biblical map is a record of the way in which God attempted to alter the consciousness of humans. Through acts in the history of Israel and in lives of the Christian community God sought to turn humanity around, to bring us to a new way of understanding our lives. Brueggemann's argument that the Bible relates a struggle between what he calls the prophetic and the royal consciousness (see chap. 3 above) demonstrates the way in which the Bible is a resource for cultural transformation. The task of prophetic ministry is to nurture, nourish, and summon forth an alternative consciousness and perception different from the consciousness and perception of the dominant culture around us.[9]

Throughout the major periods of biblical history there was a persistent effort to transform the dominant consciousness. I will sketch this effort only in its broadest outlines and thereby review much of the evidence we have treated more extensively in previous chapters.

Israel itself—the people of God—posed an alternative consciousness to the world in which it found itself (see chap. 3 above). It was a society within a society, embracing different values and a different way of perceiving reality. That difference was rooted in Israel's view of history. For it was in history, the Mosaic faith claimed, that the revelation of the divine was to be found and not in the cycles of nature.[10] But the different perspective is illustrated in other ways as well. A system of the equal distribution of land among the tribes, assuring that one never be permanently dispossessed of land expresses a unique consciousness. The cultural mentality explicit in a system of law that called for the just treatment of the deprived (see chap. 1 above) is equally unique.

In the prophets we find evidence of a stubborn call to a different consciousness. In particular, the call is to a consciousness of the nature of God and what it means to live in covenantal faithfulness. The prophets tried to reverse a particular self-perception and a God-perception that had crept into the mentality of the Israelites.[11] The prophetic critique of culture was more than a criticism of actions and the absence of actions. It was a critique of the basic values of a society, indeed, of the cultural consciousness itself.

The faithful remnant in Israel served as a summons to a new consciousness that called the whole of Israel and even the world to embrace that mentality. The best example of this are the suffering servant songs of Deutero-Isaiah (see chap. 3 above). This servant of the Lord was a model of what it meant to live with a different consciousness than that of the world. The servant consciousness perceived suffering as a means of bringing justice to the world and understood service as the ultimate response of the people of God.

The Jesus movement sought to evoke a new consciousness. It centered in the sense of the nearness of the reign of God and the implications of that for human life. The proclamation of Jesus stood in sharp contrast with the consciousness of his culture and declared that the reign of God demanded a total transformation of consciousness. That new consciousness involved a novel society in which there was care for all and total inclusiveness, especially of the marginalized (see chaps. 2 and 3 above).

Paul claimed that the gospel shattered the consciousness of social distinctions, most especially that between the Jew and the Gentile. It evoked a vision of a new society in which the Christian participated by virtue of Christ. To be "in Christ" meant for Paul the acceptance of a new consciousness that transcended the social margins of his day (see chap. 3 above).

The early church, as Luke describes it in Acts, attempted to live out a new consciousness in the society of the day. For instance, the Christian consciousness, according to Acts, was expressed in the sharing of material possessions in terms of need rather than merit or achievement. It practiced the inclusiveness of which Paul wrote, integrating within itself the two major classes of humans—Jews and Gentiles.

This new, alternative consciousness witnessed throughout the biblical faith has a consistent center. In each of the periods of the biblical history two points are consistent: the nature of the ultimate reality—the God of love and justice (a point discussed in chaps. 1 and 2 above)—and the presence of the divine that evokes something new from humans. Yahweh is present in Moses' ministry in acts of power to lead the people out of Egypt (e.g., Exodus 14), present among the people in their sojourn into Canaan (e.g., Exod. 33:7-11), and after their settlement in the promised land (e.g., Judg. 20:27). The divine presence is known to the people in "the word of the Lord" that came to and was articulated by the prophets (e.g., Hos. 1:1), in the mighty act that led them back from exile (Isa. 40:10-11), and in the law around which they built their renewed home (Neh. 8:8). God is present in Christ (e.g., John 1:1, 14), in the proclamation of the gospel (e.g., Rom. 10:8), and in the Spirit bestowed on the community (e.g., John 15:26-27). The transformation of consciousness which runs through the biblical story is connected with the presence of God—a God whose nature and will is constantly revealed. The invitation to a new consciousness is, therefore, always associated with the nearness of God. The presence of God makes the change of consciousness possible and shapes the new consciousness.

The church's role in effecting the emergence of a new cultural consciousness is found, first of all, in its proclamation in word and deed of the immanence of God. Without a radical theocentricity the church has no hope of enabling an alternative to the consciousness of the prevalent society. Our hope lies exclusively in the persistent message that God has chosen to reside among the people of God: "And the Word became flesh and lived among us . . . we have seen his glory" (John 1:14). That presence is supremely in the proclamation of the gospel and in the Sacraments of Baptism and the Eucharist, but also in the enactment of the gospel in deed. That presence is the provocation of the new consciousness which in turn makes social ministry possible. In the incarnation in Christ and the continuing incarnation of God's presence in the word and deed of the community of faith, the gradual process of the metamorphosis of our cultural mentality is generated.

The Church and Consciousness

If the Bible is a resource for the transformation of consciousness, how can the church avail itself of this resource in the effort to change the popular American mentality? Needless to say this question is not going to be answered in any detail. Indeed, this entire book is addressed to that question in some way or other, and the next chapter in particular will show how the Bible helps in the generation of a new consciousness. But some suggestions must be made here as to how we can utilize the Bible as a consciousness-changing resource in the church. These few suggestions have one purpose in mind: to stimulate the reader's reflection on what might happen in her or his own congregation.

If the proclamation of the gospel and the sacramental life of the congregation are themselves consciousness generating, why is it necessary to say more? It is necessary because the power of the immanence of God in creating a new consciousness is obviously not being unleashed in the church today. Something is inhibiting the power of the presence of God to overcome the prisons of our cultural consciousness. More, then, needs to be done to break through the self-perpetuating walls of the current American mentality.

First, intentional didactical efforts are called for. This assumes that ideas do change consciousness. It might be argued that ideas are simply interpreted and reshaped so as to fit into the current consciousness. But new thoughts and concepts have a power to smash the consciousness of a culture, to call it into question, and to judge it. Therefore, we need a dedicated effort to teach the consciousness that arises from the presence of God in Christ—to communicate the way in which the biblical faith calls forth a new way of understanding ourselves and experience. As part of this enterprise theology must be reclaimed by the people of God and taken out of its isolation from the grass roots of the church. In our idolizing of expertise we have allowed theology to become the domain of the few and denied it to the many. Consequently, theology has become threatening and foreign to too many lay persons.

Our teaching must deliberately expose the current consciousness and its differences from the biblical consciousness. In this way our teaching needs to become prophetic in the sense in which Brueggemann has defined it—challenging, exposing, and critiquing the ordinary ways in which we think. This may mean that we will need innovative teaching materials for the task.

Second, our task calls for the skillful and purposeful use of the biblical and gospel story. This is needed, because narrative changes consciousness often where ideas fail. Narrative seduces people into participation in the biblical drama and addresses such fundamental matters as cultural mentality in a subtle and indirect way. If narrative enables participation, participation facilitates the change of consciousness. Jesus models this fact for us in his use of parables as a means of teaching what otherwise would be unteachable, namely, the consciousness of the reign of God. For good reason the biblical material is made up predominantly of narratives rather than propositions. We have become preoccupied with propositional thought, this book being exhibit number one. The hope for narrative preaching and teaching is that it can break through the current consciousness of people with truth where propositional language would be simply rejected or reinterpreted to fit the current consciousness.

Finally, the new consciousness of which we have been speaking is generated when it is experienced in incarnate form. This means then that the church should begin as best it can to demonstrate an alternative consciousness. It is time, I believe, to take more seriously the idea of the church as an alternative community (cf. chap. 3 above). Insofar as the community of faith can provide an actual experience of a different consciousness, it nurtures the growth of that consciousness. Let members of the congregation witness what it means to live, for instance, as people in solidarity with others beyond the four walls of the church building. Allow people to experience the enactment of the effort to practice justice and not just charity. Give people a glimpse of what a holism might mean. This way we may let people experience what it means to live the characteristics of a new consciousness.

Through participation in a community of an alternative consciousness we may be transformed. When we experience such a consciousness we have our own mentality called into question. Unfortunately, we have effectively neutralized the power of the Bible to provide that kind of experience when we have allowed the current consciousness to make the Bible mean what suits itself. The power of the biblical word, however, makes it impossible to keep it penned up in an alien consciousness for long. With the help of one who reads with new eyes and hears with new ears, we can be led to experience the consciousness of the biblical faith once again. The interpretation of Scripture by the Christians of the third world can supply us with hearing aids and new glasses for more effective attentiveness to the biblical message.[12]

Conclusion

Until the church attends to the matter of the prevailing consciousness in America, no efforts at renewed social ministry are going to have much effect. We are trying to bail the water out of the ocean with a communion chalice. A more fundamental and frontal attack on the predominant mentality of America is needed. That attack begins and takes its orientation from the transformation that arises from the consciousness of the presence of the God of justice, but it continues in our intentional efforts to allow that new mentality to break through the walls we have put around ourselves.

But the consciousness-changing process takes another form as well. We can begin to change consciousness for ministry to society when we attend to the real and specific fears that have chained the arms and legs of the body of Christ. To those chains of fears we now turn.

Notes

1. In my opinion and to my knowledge the best and most comprehensive introduction to social ministry is Hessel, *Social Ministry*.

2. A basic and most helpful book in this matter is Berger and Luckmann, *The Social Construction of Reality*. A more recent volume that develops this

sociology of knowledge for the purposes of New Testament interpretation is Kee, *Knowing the Truth.*

3. Bellah, et al., *Habits of the Heart,* x.

4. Ibid., 191–92.

5. Ibid., 290–91.

6. This idolization was labeled, "The Triumph of the Therapeutic," in the book by that name authored by Rieff.

7. Yoder, *The Politics of Jesus,* 157–58.

8. An insightful book on views of justice is Lebacqz, *Six Theories of Justice.*

9. Brueggemann, *The Prophetic Imagination,* 13.

10. Cf. the classic statement of this perspective in Childs, *Myth and Reality.*

11. Cf. the discussion of the social change in Israel prior to the eighth century by Bright, *A History of Israel,* esp. 256–57.

12. Cf. Brown, *Unexpected News.*

6

Overcoming
the Phobias

Nothing inhibits action as much as fear. Fear can immobilize the human. It drains away our courage and our will. We have only to recall some of our own experiences of having the fear of personal rejection or loss of love deter our acting. Fear is the worst enemy of the human capacity to act.

It should not surprise us, then, to hear that fear inhibits ministry. When we turn up the volume of the congregational sounds on our imaginary stereophonic listening device, we hear those fears loudly and clearly. My thesis is simply that there is a series of fears common among members of a congregation—lay and ordained—that immobilizes us in the face of the call to ministry in society. That thesis needs to be defended only among those who have had no experience living and working within a congregation. One example will suffice. The church council tables a motion to allow a group of parents of gay and lesbian children to meet in the church building. The reason is clearly that the council members fear the possible implications of having their congregation identified with such a group. Would it mean that their church would be labeled as a congregation of gay and lesbian persons? Would there be outcries of protest from those who oppose homosexuality in any form? Would there be misunderstandings of the motives of the congregation in taking this action? It is better left undecided, they urge.

121

Theological Fear

The first class of fears we need to overcome are theological in nature. The theological fears that haunt some in a congregation, and especially clergy, have to do with the relationship between faith and works. Classical Christian thought has properly held that we are brought into a right relationship with God through faith alone apart from works (e.g., Rom. 3:28 and Gal. 2:16). God's grace alone makes our salvation possible, and everything depends on God's act on our behalf. Our own acts cannot achieve a right relationship with God, only the divine grace poured out in the person of Jesus Christ.

Clergy and lay leaders quite rightly struggle with the task of helping us learn to live our theology of grace and faith. In America it is particularly difficult for us to appropriate the implications of that theology. Ours is a "works" oriented culture—one in which it is assumed that anything we have is (or should be) the result of our hard work. It is part of the American work ethic implicit in the classic (if erroneous) American dream: Only in America can one who has nothing rise to wealth and power.

Given such a cultural atmosphere, the message of the gospel falls on unbelieving, if not deaf, ears. Leaders need to stress the doctrine of justification by grace through faith again and again, if ever they are to lead typical Americans into some degree of comprehension and—even more difficult—internalization (and living) of the doctrine. Often the task seems to be as futile as trying to build an ice sculpture in July somewhere in the deserts of Arizona.

Yet the other side of the coin is that there is an often expressed cry in middle America for the very thing the Christian view of justification offers. Not only is it the center of our faith. It answers the yearning in us all to escape the futility of trying to make ourselves acceptable through our own efforts. Not by accident are the appointment books of counselors filled to the margins in contemporary America. The emotional pains that arise from our cultural insistence on "making it on our own" are deep and lasting. We are a culture in search of unconditional love and acceptance. The search leads, we believe, to the gospel and most especially to the conviction that we are unconditionally loved and accepted by our Creator.

The nurturing of a comprehension of justification by grace through faith is fraught nonetheless by dangers. In particular there are two distortions of the doctrine that insidiously creep into the minds and emotions of people. On the one hand, the doctrine is easily misinterpreted to mean that we are relieved, even warned against good works. On the other hand, the danger is that we do not comprehend the implications of the doctrine for our own failures in ministry. Our immediate concern is how we can nurture a theological atmosphere in which faithful social ministry can take place, given the dangers on both our right and left.

Fear of Works Righteousness

Our central doctrinal view is that justification is first of all and always a matter of who God is and what God does and not what we do. But from the effort to keep this doctrine at the heart of our lives and ministry there arises an excessive fear of "works righteousness," that is, an attempt through our deeds to make ourselves righteous and thereby acceptable to God. Works righteousness is the label given the view that—however imperceptibly—holds that our efforts in doing righteousness compromise our total dependence on divine grace for a relationship with God. There is indeed a justifiable fear of such an attitude, for it violates the core of Christian faith. However, an excessive or inflated fear of works righteousness is also possible.

Such an obsession that any human deeds may lead to a works righteousness constitutes a fundamental misunderstanding of the meaning of justification. The attitude among Christians to which I refer here is one that construes any deeds of love to be fraught with danger in that they may lead us to think that we can win our acceptance in the eyes of God. Understandably, in the process of trying to enable people to comprehend the meaning of the doctrine in this cultural milieu, teachers and preachers may unintentionally nurture a fear of doing good works. In fact what we want to teach is a fear of good works done for the wrong reason, but that subtle distinction may be lost to some in their zeal to protect the doctrine of justification.

Works of righteousness, consequently, always carry the threat of enticing us into the insidious confidence that we are thereby winning favor with God. Pastors in particular may be very sensitive to the dangers of preaching the importance of service for fear of feeding the works mentality that pervades our culture. Even the risk of being interpreted as implying that our deeds of righteousness are important in our relationship with God is avoided at all cost—indeed, at the cost of failing to preach and teach the imperative of the gospel message.

Such fear of works (erga-phobia) haunts the congregation, like a ghost who only fleetingly appears now and again in the darkest of corners but whose presence is felt.

This is hardly a place to enter into a full discussion of the theological relationship between faith and works. Instead, I propose only two theses. The first is that the New Testament consistently holds that the imperative of the gospel flows directly from justification. The second is that justification itself is properly understood only in a social relationship.

We have only to read Paul's letters to see the inexorable connection between faith and works. The strongest and clearest proponent for justification by grace through faith is also the most vigorous advocate of the Christian life-style of service to others. Without exception, every one of Paul's letters contains ethical exhortations, each assuming that the Christian life is not a inner, spiritual trust of God's promise that finds no expression in moral life. One example will suffice: After building his case for justification by grace through faith in the early chapters of Romans, Paul quickly turns to the issue of the Christian life-style in chapter 6. In 12:1 he calls on his readers "to present your bodies as a living sacrifice, holy and acceptable to God which is your spiritual worship." Paul is pleading here for an understanding of the whole person living and acting by grace as an expression of worship. Many would argue even that the heart of this Pauline epistle is not the early chapters on theology but in his climatic plea that Gentiles and Jews live together at peace in the Roman congregation (Romans 15).

But it is also Paul who most succinctly and memorably states the relationship between faith and works of love. Writing to the troubled churches in Galatia, Paul is merciless in attacking a view that (apparently) had influenced the readers. It held that Christians were obliged to be circumcised and thereby take upon themselves the responsibility for obedience to the whole of the Torah (Galatians 2). For Paul circumcision had come to represent the position that humans were required to earn God's acceptance through their obedience. When Paul tries then to say what is of most importance in our relationship with God, he writes, "For in Christ Jesus neither circumcision nor uncircumcision counts for anything; the only thing that counts is faith working through love" (Gal. 5:6).

We might expect Paul simply to contrast circumcision and faith and thereby claim that faith is what matters, not circumcision. Instead, it is "faith working through love" that constitutes his characterization of the crucial Christian issue. The Greek word *energeō* means to "work, "operate" or "act." Our trust of God becomes effective or operative through love, Paul insists, and love is the distinctive mark of the Christian. Faith for Paul is not, then, an internal attitude that finds no expression in one's behavior. Rather, faith expresses itself—finds its language—in love that motivates us to act on behalf of others. Understanding this feature of Pauline thought makes 1 Cor. 13:13 comprehensible. Love is the greatest because it encompasses both faith and hope.

The New Testament evidence for the view that Paul puts so well is too abundant for us to exhaust in this discussion. However, we may note two clear examples. The first is the view of the Gospel of Matthew. Enough has already been said (see chap. 3 above) to make clear that the first evangelist propagated the necessity of a life of righteousness rooted in the teachings of Jesus himself. Furthermore Matthew understood that Christians were accountable before God for the quality of their moral lives and features the topic of judgment in the presentation of the Gospel story (e.g., 13:24-30; 18:23-35; 25:31-46). Matthew also insists that life in the kingdom means doing and not only confessing (7:21-27). Yet the first evangelist never denies the centrality of the grace of God. The parable of the workers in the vineyard is included in the Gospel of Matthew, for instance, and that parable is a vivid portrayal of the radicality of God's grace (Matt. 20:1-16). Matthew, I suggest, shared the conviction of the Pauline formulation: A right relationship with God depends on the divine grace received by a faith that operates through works of love.

The last bit of evidence appeals to the much maligned Epistle of James. This author saw the dangers implicit in a view of justification that isolated faith from works. The formulation in James may not be as satisfying as that of Paul's, but it is far more Pauline than some have held. The author is correct in the assertion "faith by itself, if it has no works, is dead" (James 2:17), if one falsely bifurcates faith and works. When the text claims that Abraham's "faith was active along with his works, and faith was brought to completion by the works" (2:22), it is not far from the Pauline formulation. If the author of James does not hold faith and works together as well as we would like and as Paul does, it is doubtless due to the polemic task the epistle undertakes. This writer was apparently trying to correct a view that took the Pauline doctrine of justification by faith as a rationale for inactivity—a condition not terribly different from the fear of works mistakenly inferred by some today.

The New Testament, therefore, is consistent in teaching that the faith God grants us and by which we accept the divine justifying grace is a trust that has an outer, active dimension, as well as an inner one. As a posture of trust on the part of the whole person, faith involves acting with love toward others even as we have been the objects of God's act of love. The New Testament grants no basis for a fear of good works, as long as they arise from the confidence that we already stand in a relationship of love with our Creator and do not need to earn that relationship.

That may be the heart of the problem. The Christian doctrine of justification by faith does not demean works of love, but it clarifies the motive for and the place of such works. Works follow justification as an expression and integral part of faith and trust. They do not precede justification as a means of attaining that kind of relationship with God. Works righteousness has not to do with deeds of love themselves but with the motivation behind the deeds. There is reason to fear nurturing works righteousness only if we do not understand the proper order of faith (grace) and works. Once the proper order is understood, works of love follow faith as surely as the shadow follows the body.[1]

Fear of good works in the doctrine of justification has no basis for still another reason. The doctrine itself has a social dimension too often overlooked. Typical of our individualistic mentality we are inclined to think of justification as a private affair between ourselves and God. It has to do, we are prone to think, only with the relationship the individual has with God. As such, then, it has no implications for the way we relate to others. This individualistic distortion of the doctrine of justification by grace through faith is part and parcel of the distortion that sees good deeds as antithetical to a justified relationship.

The New Testament does not understand justification to be a private matter between the individual and God. Increasingly Pauline scholars are stressing that its original form was far more social than individualistic. Justification or salvation addresses the "righting" of social relationships and not simply the relationship of an individual with God. To be justified refers to the state of our relationships with other people as well as with God—it has a social dimension. John Howard Yoder points out that in the New Testament, " 'Justification' is . . . in the language of Galatians the same as 'making peace' or 'breaking down the wall' in Ephesians."[2] All those expressions have to do with fundamental relationships within society. Other New Testament scholars are more and more agreeing with this view.[3]

This new sense of the social dimensions of the biblical doctrine of justification by grace through faith arises in large part from Paul's expression of the doctrine. Paul's view of justification was directed more toward social than individual relationships. The apostle was concerned to break down the barriers created between humans in the split between Gentiles and Jews, because he believed that in Christ that division was transcended (e.g., Gal. 3:28). To be justified was then to stand in right relationship with others as well as with God. The God relationship and the human relationship could no more be severed than could the love of God and others required by the great commandment (Mark 12:30-31). To be righted by God's grace is to be brought into harmony with our neighbor as well as with our God.

When understood in its New Testament form, then, the doctrine of justification in no way diminishes the call to serve our needy neighbor. On the contrary, it enhances that call. Justified by God's grace through faith and not through works means, first, trusting the divine grace through acts of love done on behalf of others, and, second, coming into a right relationship with other people. The doctrine offers no basis for fear of good works, unless those works are done out of the desire to do for ourselves what God's grace has already done.

But even if our good works are done from time to time for the wrong reason, the doctrine of justification itself allows us the freedom from excessive worry over works righteousness. To the topic of that freedom of grace we now turn.

Justification Fear

The second of our theological fears arises not so much from a misunderstanding of justification by grace through faith as from a total lack of its comprehension. The fear is that I will not be justified in God's eyes, or (more likely) that I will lose that relationship with God because of my failures. This fear of the loss of justification is rooted in a fear of the consequences of my failures.

It is a common fear among Christians. It expresses itself in an excessive care not to risk failure. Such a fear surfaces most often when the congregation is asked to venture a new program, a new form of ministry. Programs of social ministry often come up against such fear. The fear is that the program will fail, that it will prove to have been a mistake, that people will be hurt rather than helped. Or, perhaps even more common, is the fear that in taking a stand on a social issue we may be wrong. To take a stand on a social issue today is risky, because the issues are so complex. What if the stand we take is not the right one?

The fear is of failure, failure of a program or failure to be right in the stand one takes on an issue. But this fear of failure cloaks a deeper fear—fear of what the failure will mean for our relationship with God. Will God withdraw love from us because we have blundered so badly? Will our failure stretch the divine grace beyond to its limits? Will our failure somehow be punished?

We Christians want to please God—no matter that we have been told thousands of times that God is pleased with us as we are. Hence, we live with the burden of obligation we feel toward God. Perhaps we project onto our relationship with God feelings we have about our relationships with our parents. Without "psychologizing" the question, it seems that many of us have been conditioned throughout our childhood to believe that we are loved so long—and only so long—as we are good and successful. Some of us interpreted our parents' actions and attitudes to mean that their love was conditional on our good behavior. Therefore, we conclude that, if we fail, we are no longer worthy of love. Behind our fear of failure in social ministry lurks the dark shadow of doubt about our lovableness before God. Failure calls into question just how worthy we may be of the love of our Creator. In that sense, failure tests our trust of the act of God in Christ and its justifying benefits.

Once again our culture feeds our fear. Success is surely one of the major themes of our society. Young people launch a career with the desire above all else to be successful. America rewards success. The celebrity mentality of America evidences this point. The celebrity today is a person who has won success in some field. We earn our worth by succeeding, most especially in our vocations. Failure, on the other hand—be it in business, in marriage, in child rearing, in avocations, or whatever—is like a scarlet letter with which we are marked. Failure in behavior is interpreted to mean that we are failures as persons.

Rightly understood the doctrine of justification by grace through faith relieves us of fear of failure and particularly the justification fear. It does so, first of all, by assuring us that we will fail to act faithfully in every case. The doctrine of justification is linked with a particular understanding of human nature. We are creatures who are bound to fail just as surely as we are always sinful. There is no more escaping the possibility of failure than there is of escaping our humanity. Justification by faith assumes that we are the kind of creatures for whom sin and failure are natural, even when we live in a right relationship with God.

But the doctrine of justification also insists that even those failures do not endanger our relationship with God. That we are justified by grace and not by our own efforts means precisely that we are "graced" even in our failures. One who lives by grace handles failure quite differently than one whose self-worth hangs entirely on her or his degree of success. The Christian who has digested the doctrine of justification knows that when she fails God's grace does not fail her. A congregation that lives by grace knows that some of its efforts will fail but that faithfulness means trying, not succeeding. It means venturing in the confidence of the gospel and risking failure. Even if I do unintentionally begin to view my good works as earning God's favor— even if I become guilty of works righteousness—God's grace is not withdrawn from me because of such a failure.

The Christian view of justification implies that divine grace frees us from all such fear of failure. Our justification is not dependent on ourselves and our actions but on God and the divine actions. Hence we are freed to trust God and the divine forgiveness rather than our own successes. We are freed to take risks for God, because we know that failure does not mean the termination of our love relationship with our Creator. That relationship is secure because of God's faithfulness (or God's "righteousness," as Paul would say, e.g., Rom. 3:21). It is not dependent on our purity from failure.

This truth is found at the heart of what Paul meant by the freedom of the gospel about which he wrote so often. Even a hasty perusal of the Pauline letters makes it evident that Paul believed the gospel brought a new freedom. "For freedom Christ has set us free," he wrote to the Galatians amid their temptation to put themselves under the burden of the obedience to a new legalism (Gal. 5:1). "Where the Spirit . . . is, there is freedom," he counsels the Corinthians (2 Cor. 3:17). Paul believed that in Christ God was freeing humans from all that which restrained them and prevented their being the creatures God had intended. Christian liberty is freedom from the obligation that we must prove ourselves acceptable (worthy) to God. For Paul that was the essence of Christian freedom and is what he meant by speaking of freedom from the Law (e.g., Gal. 3:23-29). The gospel frees us to be who we truly are—children of God.

What then does that freedom have to say about our fear of failure? Surely it means that we are freed from concern that our failures might endanger our relationship with God. Surely it means that fear of failure is characteristic of life under the law, that is life lived as if we had to earn our approval before God. We can take risks that may entail failure. We need not be successful in order to be faithful. Specifically the freedom of the gospel offers us the liberty to venture programs in ministry that may not succeed and the independence to take stands when the clarity of truth on the issue is far from certain.

The theological fears that inhibit our ministry to society are in every case rooted in misconceptions of sound doctrine and biblical teaching. This suggests that our social ministry is rooted in careful and precise education in matters of faith and doctrine. If we can succeed in learning what it means to live as persons brought into a relationship with God through divine grace alone, then the result is a freedom from the fears that enchain our ministries.

Practical Fears

The theological fears we have just discussed can permeate the mentality of a congregation and effectively retard its efforts to minister to society. But equally threatening are a series of fears of a less theological and a more practical nature. I mean by the category of "practical fears" those that arise less from a concern about our relationship with God than from a relationship with people. They are fears of strategy—fears about what we are to do and how we are to do it. These vary in intensity and relevance, of course, among congregations, but I would venture to say that each can find representation in nearly every congregation. These phobias range from those in which there is a great deal of truth to those in which there is little or no truth. Only by understanding such fears can they be addressed, diminished, and replaced by courage.

The specific fears isolated here for discussion arise from the experience of talking with laity and clergy about the social ministry of their congregations. The fears that loom the largest in my experience are the following.

"They're Taking Over Our Church!"

An intern at a congregation, located in a neighborhood that was experiencing a great deal of change, made what he thought was an innocuous suggestion to the Committee on Evangelism. The church had erected on the lawn in front of their building a cross on the intersection of the bars of which was superimposed a red heart. On the heart were the simple words, "God love you." Because there were a good many Hispanics living within only a few blocks of the church building, the intern suggested that the message on the heart be written in Spanish as well as English. He thought that doing so would proclaim the truth of the gospel in the simplest of terms to those who read Spanish more easily than English.

The Evangelism Committee was divided on the issue and referred the decision to the church council. The question, to the surprise of both the pastor and the intern, evoked a heated debate. The arguments against the action included the insistence that the church must encourage the Hispanics to learn English and not cater to their reliance on their native language. Soon the discussion began to focus on the trend toward multilingual education in America. The motion to add the Spanish to the sign finally failed, much to the dismay of the still surprised pastor and her intern.

This incident suggests one of the fears many feel when a congregation reaches out in service to those who are different from the majority of the members of the congregation (or at least from those members of the congregation who hold power). We have heard the fear expressed in these words: "They're taking over our church!" Serve those who are of a different economic, racial, national, or class background, and you may find them entering the congregation and assuming prominence there.

The fear seems to arise from two sources. First, it is a basic fear of change but specifically a fear of the change of the homogeneous character of the congregation. A congregation takes on character shaped by its constituents, and members of the congregation grow comfortable with that character. More often than not a congregation is comprised of people who share status in an economic class, race, nationality, and even ethnic background. It tends to become what Bellah and his associates labeled a "life-style enclave."[4] The congregation is inclined to become homogeneous, and the threat to that homogeneity is frightening to many. It changes the cozy "family" character of a congregation to have new people who are unlike the longstanding members. Basically the fear of the congregation becoming more pluralistic is another form of the fear rooted deeply in human personality, namely, the fear of change. But the fear of change seems particularly acute with regard to the church where people come to look for and expect stability amid the tidal waves of change in society as a whole.

Would it be reassuring to know that the earliest Christian congregations, as well as the people of Israel, experienced the same kind of fear? Israel feared losing its identity if its ethnic purity was not maintained. The Book of Ezra witnesses to the fact that the intermarriage of Jew and Gentile constituted a threat to the identity of the people after the return from exile, so that a movement to forbid such marriages and compel their dissolution was begun (Ezra 9 and 10). Israel was afraid of the change that pluralistic families would bring.

But the early Christians, too, struggled with the same issue. First, it appears to have been the issue of whether Gentiles were to be allowed to enter the earliest church comprised solely of Jews who had accepted the gospel. The agony this question caused the New Testament church is evident in Paul's account of a meeting in Jerusalem (Galatians 2). The question continued to plague the church, it appears, as Christians of both Jewish and gentile backgrounds tried to learn to live together in faith, as Romans 9–11 indicates. Then there is evidence that socioeconomic pluralism troubled the New Testament church. For instance, the Epistle of James testifies to the possibility that the congregation(s) addressed in that writing were trying to preserve a community that tended to exclude the poor (e.g., 2:1-7).

While the human struggle to live in a pluralistic community of faith is evident in the Bible, so too is the persistent call to that kind of life. Galatians 3:28 might have been a pronouncement used on the occasion of baptism. It declares that Christian faith leaps the boundaries humans create among themselves and that consequently the Christian community is pluralistic by its very nature (cf. 1 Cor. 12:13; Col. 3:11).

If the social ministry of the church threatens the comfortable homogeneity of the congregation, then it enables us to be the community the gospel calls us to be. If it means that "those people are going to take over our church," perhaps that is what is required by life in the body of Christ in this particular time and place.

But the fear that a different kind of people are going to be attracted to the congregation by an effective social ministry also entails another basic fear, namely, the loss of power. Psychological theorists have long said that the quest for power is at least one of the primary forces in human personality. It comes as no surprise that many people are actively involved in a congregation because it gives them a place to exercise power. Those council members who objected to adding Spanish to the sign in front of the church building were less concerned with the preservation of English as the sole language in America than they were with their own positions of power in the congregation. To make the church attractive to Spanish-speaking people in the neighborhood entailed the risk of having their power usurped by new people.

The social ministry of the church aims at the empowerment of all people, particularly those who have been robbed of power by social structures. In principle, therefore, ministry to societal needs poses a threat to all who relish their power. When it succeeds, social ministry requires a new sharing of power with those who have been disempowered. Therefore, those concerned with strengthening social ministry must take seriously the threat such power sharing poses for members of a congregation and for all with power in society.

Yet the biblical message is clear. Those who align themselves with the God of Abraham and Sarah, Moses, Jesus, Mary, and Paul abandon their thirst for power, for there is but one power—God. Moreover, true power is found for the Christian not in authority and status but in service and obedience. James, John, and their mother painfully learned this in an incident that was engraved on early Christian memory so that it is found in an early strata of Christian tradition (Mark 10:35-45; Matt. 20:20-28; Luke 22:24-27). In response to their request for positions of authority Jesus insists that among his disciples there shall be no exercise of authority. Rather, "whoever wishes to be great among you must be your servant, and whoever wishes to be first among you must be your slave; just as the Son of Man came not to be served but to serve" (Matt. 20:26-28).

The fear of the loss of power is overcome finally only by understanding that the exercise of authority has no place in the community of faith but only servanthood. The inclusion of those who do not share the same background with the majority of the members of the congregation is a fearful experience. Those fears need to be acknowledged and named. They also need to be addressed in the context of the biblical faith and its understanding of the community of Christian faith.

"The Job Is too Big for Us!"

Another expression that is heard when one listens carefully is the fear that a particular social ministry task is too much for a congregation to undertake. Sometimes it is explicitly stated; more often it is sensed under and behind the reservations that are verbalized. Imagine a congregation of two hundred relatively active members undertaking the task of overcoming years and maybe centuries of racial discrimination in housing in its community! Who would not say, "The job is too big for us"?

This is one of those fears founded in reality. It is true that most social ministry tasks are "too big" for the congregation. The church's effort to alter social realities is a phenomenal undertaking, but discipleship itself is a phenomenal undertaking. It would help to understand the foundation of this fear in at least two of its aspects.

The first component of the fear that "the job is too big for us" is the fact that social problems today are so very complex (cf. chap. 5 above). A social ministry task is often thought to be "too big" in part because it involves a complex of issues. Congregational leaders are intimidated by social problems. It is as if we stand at the plate with the bat on our shoulder facing the best pitcher in the American League. What chance do we have?

One salutary and commendable response to the complexity of social problems today is in "networking"—linking congregations in an effort to respond to specific social needs. But it may also have some dangerous results. As those networks become institutionalized, congregations may tend to surrender responsibility to the "experts" and the agencies that supposedly understand the maze through which one must travel to cure a social ill. As the church develops agencies and institutions to meet the needs of society, congregations may be increasingly content to abdicate responsibility for social needs and offer token support to those agencies and institutions as their contribution to the cause. While the church needs just such organizations geared up to work effectively on behalf of social service, one of the dangers of the movement is that social ministry becomes the business not of the congregation but those organizations. Social ministry then becomes a special interest that is beyond the ordinary congregational member.[5]

The New Testament speaks a clear and challenging word to the fear that the job may be too big for the congregation. That word is simply "empowerment." The earliest Christians experienced an empowerment as a result of the gospel that they could only attribute to the force of the Spirit of God in their midst. The Acts of the Apostles narrates that sense of divine empowerment on page after page. The early band of Christians dared to believe that they were called to transform the world of their time. Surely they thought, "The job is too big for us!" But yet they believed it was their mission. What continually surprised them was that they had power to do the unthinkable. Luke makes clear in the structure of the narrative of Acts that that power came from God and was the source of the effectiveness of the church.

The social ministry of the church begins on the premise that "The job is too big for us" and depends entirely on the empowerment of God. In this case we do not deny the reality that produces its fruit of fear. But we do deny that the fear is insurmountable for one simple reason: the Holy Spirit and its power. Unless the congregation takes seriously the message of Acts, unless it can believe that there is a divine empowering possible, there is no antidote for this fear.

But the fear, "The job is too big for us," often betrays another foundational stone that rests less on reality than despair. The despair is born of a social fatalism that is common in many circles. You and I have heard it articulated time and again. Humans being what they are, there will always be poverty, homelessness, discrimination, neglect of the elderly, and so forth. There is nothing one can finally do to alter the nature of the situation. We are counseled by these modern-day fatalists to accept the reality of what will always be. I was trying to convince a group of middle-class college students of the need to deal with the rising rate of poverty in America and to initiate some sharing of the wealth of the affluent. One student spoke for several in the group, stating that the wealthy will never let go of what they have earned through their efforts, and that there is no possibility of appealing to the generosity of the haves for the sake of the have-nots.

Fatalism was no stranger to the first-century Greco-Roman world. Some would argue that fatalism in one form or another was the prevalent view of the inhabitants of that first-century world. The rise of the Christian movement was a frontal attack on just such a world view. Nolan suggests that fatalism is a persistent view with no limitations to any one period of history. Fatalism is always the expression of people "who do not really believe in the power of God, people who do not really hope for what God has promised." Jesus' ministry on the other hand, says Nolan, awakened faith in just such people of the time, and that faith overthrew fatalism: "Wherever the general atmosphere of fatalism had been replaced by an atmosphere of faith, the impossible began to happen."[6]

Most of us know the experience of the fatalistic feeling. We have all felt at one point or another that there was no power mighty enough to effect change in what seemed to us the inevitability of the present situation. Fatalism always evidences the failure of faith, the demise of confidence in the power of God. It is the confession of the ones of "little faith." Social ministry begins and ends in the expression of faith and confidence in the power of God to do exceedingly more than we can do. The nurture of faith is always the nurture of ministry, not least of all the ministry to society. Only with the faith that denies the god of fatalism its reign can we experience the power that emboldens us to think that the problem is not necessarily too big for us, however small we are.

"People Won't Like This!"

Social ministry often proves to be controversial in a congregation. This may be so for two different reasons, depending on the particular program under consideration. First, there is difference of opinion about how certain problems should be treated. A case in point is a community food program. No one could disagree with the idea of offering food to the hungry, but when it was discovered that certain kinds of people were to be fed through the program, opposition arose. The opponents did not want any person suspected of laziness to benefit from the program. It was, they argued, for the worthy, those who by sheer and demonstrable misfortune were in dire need of food. How a program as innocuous as feeding the hungry is to be administered can prove to be controversial. The case was similar in the effort of one congregation to secure support for a peace march in their community. The march was organized by those opposed to nuclear weapons. Others who believed in a strong national defense objected so vigorously that the church board canceled the march. In these cases it is not the principle (feeding the hungry or attaining world peace) but the practice or strategy (feeding any one who is hungry or attaining peace through disarmament) that provokes differences of opinion.

The second reason controversy swirls around ministry to societal needs is that some issues themselves are controversial. Today congregations are discovering just how controversial a ministry to gay and lesbian persons is and even how difficult it is to attain consent to act on behalf of those afflicted with AIDS. Two decades ago U.S. participation in Viet Nam tore congregations apart. Some issues do not present themselves in a way that makes a single, commonly held principle absolutely clear. Ministering to persons involved in such an issue is bound to stir controversy.

Perhaps most and always controversial is the ministry of advocacy. Advocacy is an important part of the church's ministry to society that purports to speak on behalf of others, whose voices may not be heard in the places of power. It attempts to come to the side of others in need to promote reform that will enhance their welfare. But advocacy suffers from a bad reputation in the minds of some. It is associated, I assume, with advocacy on behalf of those whose lifestyle or stance is regarded as wrong or even sinful. Advocacy, furthermore, is associated with political matters. Much advocacy is done through the legislative systems of our nation. For the church to speak on behalf of others for legislation seems to some to violate the old adage not to mix politics and religion.

In and of itself controversy does not seem like such a undesirable thing. Indeed, in a congregation controversy can provoke discussion and the search for clarity on important questions, as well as the implications of the gospel for contemporary problems. But many congregational leaders want to avoid controversy at all costs. If there are persons who will not be pleased with the church's ministry in a certain area, leaders may shy away from moving toward that ministry even when they themselves favor it. It is not uncommon for a committee to be enthusiastic about a proposal until someone suggests that this or that prominent family in the congregation will be opposed to the action.

There sometimes is a desire to please everyone as much of the time as possible. This desire arises in some cases in the effort to keep major contributors to the church happy and in other cases to please the "pillars" of the congregation—in both cases to comply with the wishes of the powerful. But most often the desire to maintain "peace" in a congregation is paramount in the minds of many. This image of the comfortable community, living harmoniously together, motivates the desire not to offend anyone. The problem is further augmented by the lack of adequate skills in conflict management when controversy does occur.

The biblical witness is clear on this matter of avoiding controversy and keeping the peace. From what we know of the history of Israel and the early church there were frequent differences of opinion and controversy within these religious communities. The Old Testament prophets are in nearly every case controversial figures—persons who stood for unpopular views. One need only to think of Jeremiah, who suffered because of his open and vocal stand on any number of issues (e.g., Jeremiah 27), or Isaiah who had to oppose a political alliance that had widespread support (Isaiah 7). In the New Testament the story is little different. The Christian writings betray a diversity of views on a number of issues and evidence a great deal of controversy. Paul was surely a controversial figure among the Christians at Corinth, and he had to go to great lengths to defend himself (e.g., 2 Corinthians 1–9). Although Luke works hard to present the image of the early church as a unified community, the sense of historical accuracy required the narrating of several incidents of division and controversy (e.g., Acts 6:1-7; 15:36-41).

The church lived with controversy within itself, but differences of opinion did not compromise the sense of Christian solidarity. Paul and Barnabas parted ways over John Mark (Acts 15:36-41), but that did not mean that Paul and Barnabas each disavowed the genuineness of the Christian commitment of the other. There was a unity within the diversity of views. There was a sense that the body of Christ was inclusive enough to contain people who thought differently about important matters of mission and ministry.

For social ministry to be effective there needs to be a sense of acceptance of diversity of opinion. Our unity in Christ ought to hold us together when our views of social issues tend to separate us. That sense of community should be nurtured for the sake of the ministry of the church. A congregation that has a strong corporate identity will not be afraid of controversy but will understand the positive role of controversy and the fact that it need not splinter the congregation.

"We'll Help the Wrong People!"

How often the church is fearful that its social programs are going to be abused. It happens so often that a well-designed proposal flounders on the fear that the wrong people will be served by it. The really needy won't be helped, it is feared, only the "freeloaders."

The weakness of this fear resides in a question: Who are the "wrong people"? Below the surface the statement of fear, "We're going to be helping the wrong people," is an assertion that some people are worthy of our help, while others are not. There is in the statement an implicit emphasis on the word "wrong." That is to say, some people are wrong because they have not earned the right to be helped. The fear betrays the mentality of achieved worth, not intrinsic worth (cf. chap. 5 above).

How curious it is that Jesus never once asked someone in need to demonstrate that they were worthy of his help. He never examined the individual's degree of worthiness; he never withheld his healing, his exorcism, or even his forgiveness after having found a person undeserving. And how often Jesus was criticized for serving or even associating with those considered by his society to be the wrong people (e.g., Luke 7:36-50). He served as we are called to serve. People who are in need for whatever reason deserve aid simply because they are people.

But the fear of helping the "wrong people" also assumes that we cannot afford to take the risk of being misused. In this reservation resides a concern that a program of social service will suffer abuse, that certain people will take advantage of it. The fear is that the church will not be able to avoid the risk of being "ripped off" by the unscrupulous. Programs of social ministry do need to be wisely and realistically conceived and administered. On that all can agree. One food pantry simply kept records of those who availed themselves of its service. It did so less to prevent the habitual user than to make sure that as many of the needy as possible were assisted. Prudence is demanded, but still, the congregation needs to understand that one of the costs of serving the needy is the possibility of being used. Such is the risk we take not because we want to encourage those whose morality allows them to abuse a social service, but because we want to serve the needy.

I wonder about the story of the healing of the ten lepers in Luke 17:11-19. I wonder less about the reasons for the lack of gratitude on the part of the nine who did not return or about what gift the one leper had that led him to return to thank Jesus. I wonder more that Jesus did not at that point despair over human nature and retire from the ministry! While Luke records Jesus' disappointment ("Were not ten cleansed?"), the evangelist also reports that Jesus continued his ministry of healing in the very next chapter (18:35-43). Jesus did not condition his ministry by protecting himself against those who would abuse his power. He simply served human need when he encountered it.

"We're going to be helping the wrong people!" Yes, possibly in the process of serving the needy, there will be some who will not treat our efforts with respect. But that's okay. The needy will be served. Yes, possibly some will, by our standards, be more "worthy" of help than others. But that's okay. The needy will be served.

"Is This Our Mission?"

The most insidious of the fears that arise within the congregation regarding social ministry is the concern that the church's business is really not in ministry to social needs but spiritual needs. This is most often expressed in the slogan, "Evangelism, not social ministry, is the task of the church." The fear is that in addressing social needs the church neglects its more vital task of proclaiming the gospel to all people. This fear evokes vigorous debate between proponents of evangelism on the one hand and social ministry on the other.

There are two fallacious divisions made in the thinking of those who would foster this fear. The first is the division between evangelism and social ministry. Such a division demonstrates a misconception of both dimensions of the ministry of the church. In modern times the church has created these neat little organizational categories of evangelism, stewardship, social ministry, worship, and so forth. Such categories are functionally useful as a way of dividing responsibilities and thereby assuring that the ministry of the church is effective and complete. But they are little more than that. Any pastor or lay leader who has worked with the total program of a congregation knows that the lines between the various divisions of duties are tenuous at best and more likely arbitrary. Yet we tend to enshrine our organizational charts and believe that they must be found somewhere in Scripture.

The truth is that there are no such divisions to be found in the ministry of the earliest Christian churches as they are reflected in the New Testament. The mission of the church was single and unified. What we call evangelism and social ministry are both part of that single mission. As we have observed, Jesus sent the disciples out to heal and proclaim the kingdom (Luke 10:9; Matt. 10:7). It is interesting that Luke has that order—heal and proclaim—while Matthew has the reverse order—proclaim and heal—as if the order did not matter in the least.

We cannot justifiably separate these two artificial categories of mission, for social ministry may be evangelical and evangelism may be social. Social ministry is a means by which the good news of the gospel is proclaimed and to which people are invited to respond. When ministry to social needs is done clearly in the name of Christ and with the motivation of Christian love made explicit, the evangelical task is performed as surely as when verbal witness is made to one whose life is engulfed in guilt.[7]

The second false division underlying a fear that the church may abandon its true mission is between the spiritual and the physical or social needs of humans. It may be that this dichotomy really lurks beneath the division of evangelism and social ministry. The entire discussion of this volume has had as one of its agendas to demonstrate how this polarization of the spiritual from the physical is not characteristic of the biblical witness, so further exploration of the weaknesses of the separation would be redundant. Suffice it to say again that the divine care for human existence is holistic and that the faithful ministry of the church is called to be equally holistic in its concern.

The fear that "we're neglecting the real mission of the church!" is furthest from the truth. Indeed, it is the case that ministry to societal conditions is an integral part (but not the whole) of the real mission of the church.

Conclusion

The mission of the church is encumbered with human fears, including fears of both a theological and a practical kind. We are indeed a fearful people, for life in society evokes the most fundamental kinds of fears we have. Most are ill-founded, even if they are as real as any human emotion.

It is interesting that the author of the First Epistle of John sensed the reality of human fear and its destructive power for Christian life. It may be that those who had separated themselves from the community to which this author wrote were stirring fear among those who had remained part of the parent church. For whatever reason 1 John attempts to assure its readers of the certainty of God's love. If we then respond to that love by loving God and others, we have nothing to fear in the day of judgment. "There is no fear in love, but perfect love casts out fear. For fear has to do with punishment, and he who fears is not perfected in love" (1 John 4:18).[8]

Fear is always an expression of the uncertainty of love; it is always rooted in an anxiety of punishment. The final solution to fear is not, then, an argument of any kind or a demonstration of the truth of the biblical witness. The final solution to the fears of social ministry are not found in the discussion just completed. Fear's ultimate antidote lies in the acceptance of a love that neutralizes the dread of punishment, either human or divine. Let that love be nurtured among us, so that fear may subside and the energies for ministry be freed!

Notes

1. The metaphor comes from Luther's statement in his lectures on Isaiah: "For faith is followed by works as the body is followed by its shadow." Quoted

in the seminal book by Forell, *Faith Active in Love*, 56. Forell makes clear that
for all of his emphasis on justification by grace through faith alone Luther
never understood faith to have no expression in works of love.

2. Yoder, *The Politics of Jesus*, 225. Cf. the whole of Yoder's provocative
discussion of justification, 215–232.

3. For example, Stendahl, *Paul Among Jews and Gentiles;* Dahl, "The Doctrine
of Justification," 95–120; and Sanders, *Paul and Palestinian Judaism.* The
neglect of the social dimension of justification is due in large part to the false
dichotomy between individuality and corporality we have imposed on the
biblical writings (see chap. 5 above). Again Yoder is helpful when he suggests
that the tradition in the church asks us to choose between the individual and
the social. He points out, however, that "Jesus doesn't know anything about
radical personalism" and that the image of Jesus as a radical individualist is
anachronistic—entirely out of tune with the semitic mentality of the historical
Jesus. (Yoder, *Politics of Jesus*, 113–14).

4. Bellah et al., *Habits of the Heart*, 71–75.

5. Cf. the excellent volume by McCurley, *The Social Ministry of the Church*,
esp. chap. 5.

6. Nolan, *Jesus Before Christianity*, 32–33.

7. For a different but effective discussion of the relationship between ministry to social needs and evangelism cf. Mott, *Biblical Ethics and Social Change*,
chap. 6.

8. Cf. Kysar, *I, II, III John*, 98–102.

A Brief Theology
of Mission

This sketch of the biblical roots and practical directions for social ministry is yet incomplete. Perhaps we have left unexpressed the most fundamental biblical foundation for our mission to society and the implications it has for the practical way in which that mission is carried out. This conclusion will try to set social ministry in the broader scope of the mission of the church and then offer some concluding reflections.

No argument for the biblical mandate for the social ministry of the church can succeed unless it is set within the context of the way in which humans have been enlisted in a divine enterprise. While that theme was one of the subjects of chapter 3, it remains for us to examine even more carefully a passage alluded to there, namely, John 20:19-23. In that passage the mission of the church is explicated with a clarity we need to understand.

In a vivid scene the fourth evangelist reports that the resurrected Christ sent the disciples forth in their mission. The sequence of the words of Jesus in that narrative is far from accidental and forms a pattern that outlines in miniature a theology of mission. The risen Christ appears to the disciples behind closed doors. He first greets them with the words, "Peace be with you" (v. 19). Then, after demonstrating that he is indeed their crucified Lord (v. 20), he repeats his greeting of peace (v. 21). Next Jesus declares their mission with the words, "As the Father has sent me, so I send you" (v. 21), followed by this: "When he had said this, he breathed on them and said to them, 'Receive the Holy Spirit. If you forgive the sins of any, they are forgiven them; if you retain the sins of any, they are retained'" (vs. 21-23).

The fourth evangelist has structured a narrative rich with meaning for the contemporary church and its mission. The whole of the mission of the church is undertaken within the context of the risen Christ. We are in mission because we believe that this Jesus of Nazareth was not overcome by the forces of opposition, even the act of his execution. Our Christ is a living Lord, whose victory over death makes our efforts possible. The enigmatic triumph of God in suffering and death both necessitates our suffering service and provides us with a vision of the possibilities of service.

But the risen Christ offers "peace." Peace in the Fourth Gospel is not the passive contentment that we often intend in our contemporary use of the word. It is not the peace that the world gives (John 14:27). It is rather the peace that we have with God, with ourselves, and with others because of the revelation of God's nature and will in Christ. It is another word for salvation or justification—another way of imaging the intention of God for humanity as that intention is enacted in the incarnation. The mission of the church is done within the context and as a result of the act of God that makes possible peace with our Creator, ourselves, and others. Any effort to do ministry before or aside from the fundamental experience of the peacemaking activity of God is futile and erroneously undertaken. We can be in mission because God has been in mission to us, just as we can love others only because we have first been the objects of divine love in Christ (1 John 4:19).

But the peace the resurrected Christ offers is not a self-contained condition. The offer of peace is followed in our text with the mandate to mission: "As the Father has sent me, even so I send you." The peacemaking God now beckons the peaceful into responsibility. That the disciples are sent as Jesus himself was sent is pregnant with meaning. In chapter 3 I pointed out a segment of that meaning: Both the motivation and the purpose for the divine sending of Jesus is love (e.g., John 3:16). Therefore, the mission of the church arises from the love God has for creation and the purpose of its mission is to love, even as Jesus' life and ministry was comprised of love.

But, further, Jesus was God's agent in the world for the world's redemption. The agent, however, is identified in the Gospel of John with the Sender (1:1-18). The agent of God's redemptive undertaking is one with God, indeed none other than God. If the church is sent as Jesus was sent, then the community of believers is to be the incarnation of the divine will, even as Jesus was the incarnation of that will. The mission of the church, yes, is to be the agency of the divine purpose. But that does not stop at the point of doing; it equally entails being. The mission of the church is, yes, to proclaim the gospel, but also to be the gospel. Mission may never be delimited to program, for it is the character of those who carry out the program that comprises mission as surely as does the program itself. What is suggested by this mission reading of John 20:10-23 is like the image of the body that Paul uses for the church (e.g., Rom. 12:3-8; 1 Cor. 12:12-31). The church is the "human body" by which God continues to pursue the divine purpose even as that purpose was once decisively sought in the body of Jesus.

Such a concept of our mission is terrifying. And rightly so—there should always be about our sense of mission a consciousness of inadequacy and even timidity. Yet the final step in the commissioning of the disciples in John 20 addresses that very terror. The offer of peace has been followed by the commission, and the commission is now followed by the gift of power for the mission. John 20:22 is the Johannine version of the Pentecost, the bestowal of the Holy Spirit. The breath of Jesus is the Holy Spirit (the *parakletos*) promised to the disciples in the farewell discourses of chapters 14–16. That Spirit enables the people of God to undertake their mission. The divine power alone gives the courage and the ability to be sent as God sent Jesus. No mission of the church that conceives itself as independent of the power of the Spirit is true or even possible.

Finally, the commissioning of the disciples for mission involves authorization. Whatever the difficulties of John 20:23, it is clear that the gift of the Spirit means that the disciples are given a divine authority—an authority that is not theirs by nature but only by grace. As the Johannine Jesus acted and spoke with the authority of the divine Parent, even so the church now in its mission acts and speaks on behalf of God. This does not mean that we are freed of the possibility of error, but only that we are called to do faithfully what God has done in Christ. The church's mission is undertaken with assurance that it carries the authorization of God.[1]

Peace, mission, empowerment, and authorization offered by the risen Christ. The ministry to society finds its place within that mini-theology of mission. This is our rationale for daring to believe that we must act as Jesus acted in compassion for those in need. The mission framework means that our social ministry is done because God has made peace for us, empowered us with the divine Spirit, and authorized our efforts on behalf of others. Social ministry finds its reason for being in the sending of the disciples, and that sending is understood only in analogy with the divine sending of Jesus himself.

Perhaps social ministry has tended to be conceived outside of this kind of theology of mission. In the minds of many, evangelistic efforts arise within such a framework as we have tried to elucidate here while social ministry is conceived of as falling on the perimeters of this framework, if not entirely outside of them. But if our mission is singular and holistic, as I have tried to argue, then social ministry is integral to the mission on which Jesus sent the disciples. "Called to care" is the conception of our ministry to society.

The social ministry of the church, I suggest, is founded on the sending of all disciples in the love that characterized the divine sending of Jesus. The roots of social ministry are in the biblical images of God, the believing community and discipleship, and God's future for humanity. The Bible offers guidance in the general task of transforming the consciousness of the church and society and in the overcoming of fears that hamper the social dimension of the church's mission.

We cannot pretend that, after Pastor Johnson has taught her Bible study on the mission of the church, her congregation will spring eagerly into the task of feeding the hungry of the community. Surely the task of nurturing a sense of the whole mission of the church as it is described in the biblical witness is an ongoing one that requires years of preaching, teaching, and personal witness. We cannot claim an instant transformation of the congregation, once the biblical study is done. But we can claim that a better understanding of the biblical witness is the point of beginning. Only with a biblical foundation can social ministry be effective and faithful to its peculiar Christian character. With that foundation we can see that social ministry needs more than a basic humanitarianism or a simple impulse toward kindness in relationship to others.

Congregational leaders—ordained and lay—are mandated with the task of seeing that biblical foundation explicated again and again in the life of a congregation. It needs to permeate not only the teaching ministry of the church, its preaching, but also its own administrative life. Unless the whole mission of the church, including social ministry, is articulated and presupposed in the total congregational life, the church can never be faithful to its calling.

Finally it is that sense of having been sent, of being commissioned, and of being designated envoys of God's care and compassion that makes social ministry even conceivable. Like every aspect of the ministry of the church, our mission to society arises from the consciousness that we are sent, even as God sent Jesus into the world. We are called to care, even as we have been the objects of God's care for us.

Notes

1. This interpretation of the passage is suggested in my commentary on John 20:19-23. Kysar, *John*, 302–5.

Bibliography

Beker, J. Christiaan. *Paul the Apostle: The Triumph of God in Life and Thought.* Philadelphia: Fortress Press, 1980.
————. *Paul's Apocalyptic Gospel. The Coming Triumph of God.* Philadelphia: Fortress Press, 1982.
————. *The Triumph of God. The Essence of Paul's Thought.* Philadelphia: Fortress Press, 1990.
Bellah, Robert, et al. *Habits of the Heart: Individualism and Commitment in American Life.* Berkeley: University of California Press, 1985.
Berger, Peter L. and Luckmann, Thomas. *The Social Construction of Reality.* Garden City, NY.: Doubleday, 1966.
Berkhof, Hendrik. *Christ and the Powers.* Scottdale, Penn.: Herald Press, 1962.
Birch, Bruce C. *What Does the Lord Require? The Old Testament Call to Social Witness.* Philadelphia: Westminster Press, 1985.
Boerma, Conrad. *The Rich, the Poor—and the Bible.* Philadelphia: Westminster Press, 1979.
Bright, John. *A History of Israel.* 2d ed. Philadelphia: Westminster Press, 1972.
Brown, Raymond E. *The Birth of the Messiah: A Commentary on the Infancy Narratives in Matthew and Luke.* New York: Doubleday, 1977.
Brown, Robert McAfee. *Unexpected News: Reading the Bible with Third World Eyes.* Philadelphia: Westminster Press, 1984.

149

Brueggemann, Walter. *The Land*. Philadelphia: Fortress Press, 1977.

———. *The Prophetic Imagination*. Philadelphia: Fortress Press, 1978.

Caird, G. B. *The Revelation of St. John the Divine*. New York: Harper & Row, 1966.

Carlston, Charles. "Proverbs, Maxims, and the Historical Jesus." *Journal of Biblical Literature* 99 (1980): 95–96.

Cassidy, Richard J. *Jesus, Politics and Society*. Maryknoll, N.Y.: Orbis Books, 1978.

Charles, R. H. *The Revelation of St. John*. 2 vols. Edinburgh: T and T Clark, 1920.

Childs, Brevard S. *Myth and Reality in the Old Testament*. London: SCM Press, 1960.

Collins, Adela Yarbro. *Crisis and Catharsis: The Power of the Apocalypse*. Philadelphia: Westminster Press, 1984.

Collins, John J. *The Apocalyptic Imagination*. New York: Crossroads, 1984.

Dahl, Nils Alstrup. "The Doctrine of Justification: Its Social Function and Implications." *Studies in Paul*. Minneapolis: Augsburg, 1977.

Donahue, John R. *The Gospel in Parables: Metaphor, Narrative, and Theology in the Synoptic Gospels*. Philadelphia: Fortress Press, 1988.

Dupont-Sommer, A. *The Essene Writings from Qumran*. New York: World, 1962.

Fiorenza, Elisabeth Schüssler. *The Book of Revelation: Justice and Judgment*. Philadelphia: Fortress Press, 1985.

———. *In Memory of Her: A Feminist Theological Reconstruction of Christian Origins*. New York: Crossroads, 1984.

Ford, J. Massyngbaerde. "Reconciliation and Forgiveness in Luke's Gospel." *Political Issues in Luke-Acts*, ed. Richard J. Cassidy and Philip J. Scharper, 80–98. Maryknoll, N.Y.: Orbis Books, 1983.

Forell, George W. *Faith Active in Love*. Minneapolis: Augsburg, 1954.

Fretheim, Terence. *The Suffering of God: An Old Testament Perspective*. Philadelphia: Fortress Press, 1984.

Gottwald, Norman. *The Hebrew Bible.—A Socio-Literary Introduction*. Philadelphia: Fortress Press, 1985.

———. *The Tribes of Yahweh*. Maryknoll, N.Y.: Orbis Books, 1979.

Hanson, Paul D. *The Dawn of Apocalyptic: The Historical and Sociological Roots of Jewish Apocalyptic Eschatology*. Philadelphia: Fortress Press, 1975.

Hanson, Paul D., ed. *Visionaries and Their Apocalypses*. Philadelphia: Fortress Press, 1983.

Hengel, Martin. *Property and Riches in the Early Church*. Philadelphia: Fortress Press, 1974.

Hessel, Dieter T. *Social Ministry*. Philadelphia: Westminster Press, 1982.

Jeremias, Joachim. *The Central Message of the New Testament*. New York: Charles Scribner's Sons, 1965.

————. *Jerusalem in the Time of Jesus*, 3d ed. Philadelphia: Fortress Press, 1967.

————. *New Testament Theology*. Vol. 1. New York: Charles Scribner's Sons, 1971.

————. *The Prayers of Jesus*. London: SCM Press, 1967. Philadelphia: Fortress Press, 1967.

Kee, Howard Clark. *Knowing the Truth: A Sociological Approach to New Testament Interpretation*. Minneapolis: Fortress Press, 1989.

Kingsbury, Jack Dean. *The Christology of Mark's Gospel*. Philadelphia: Fortress Press, 1983.

Kraus, Hans-Joachim. *Theology of the Psalms*. Minneapolis: Augsburg, 1986.

Krodel, Gerhard. *Revelation*. Augsburg Commentary on the New Testament. Minneapolis: Augsburg, 1989.

Kysar, Myrna and Robert. *The Asundered: Biblical Teachings on Divorce and Remarriage*. Atlanta: John Knox Press, 1978.

————. *Proclamation: Lent Series C*. Philadelphia: Fortress Press, 1988.

Kysar, Robert. *I, II, III John*. Augsburg Commentary on the New Testament. Minneapolis: Augsburg, 1986.

————. *John*. Augsburg Commentary on the New Testament. Minneapolis: Augsburg, 1986.

Lebacqz, Karen. *Six Theories of Justice*. Minneapolis: Augsburg, 1986.

Limburg, James. *The Prophets and the Powerless*. Atlanta: John Knox Press, 1977.

Longenecker, Richard N. *New Testament and Social Ethics for Today*. Grand Rapids: William B. Eerdmans, 1984.

McCurley, Foster R. *The Social Ministry of the Church*. Chicago: The Division for Social Ministry Organizations, Evangelical Lutheran Church in America, 1989.

McCurley, Foster R. and Reumann, John. *Witness of the Word: A Biblical Theology of the Gospel*. Philadelphia: Fortress Press, 1986.

McFague, Sallie. *Metaphorical Theology: Models of God in Religious Language*. Philadelphia: Fortress Press, 1982.

Moltmann, Jürgen. *The Crucified God: The Cross of Christ as the Foundation and Criticism of Christian Theology*. New York: Harper & Row, 1974.

————. *The Theology of Hope: On the Ground and the Implications of a Christian Eschatology.* New York: Harper & Row, 1967.

Mott, Stephen Charles. *Biblical Ethics and Social Change.* New York: Oxford University Press, 1982.

Mounce, Robert H. *The Book of Revelation.* Grand Rapids: William B. Eerdmans, 1977.

Mowinckel, Sigmund. *He That Cometh.* New York: Abingdon Press, n. d.

Myers, Ched. *Binding the Strong Man: A Political Reading of Mark's Story of Jesus.* Maryknoll, N.Y.: Orbis Books, 1988.

Nolan, Albert. *Jesus Before Christianity.* Maryknoll, N.Y.: Orbis Books, 1976.

North, C. R. *The Suffering Servant in Deutero-Isaiah.* London: Oxford University Press, 1948.

Pilgrim, Walter E. *Good News to the Poor: Wealth and Poverty in Luke-Acts.* Minneapolis: Augsburg, 1981.

Porteous, Norman W. *Daniel.* Philadelphia: Westminster Press, 1965.

Rieff, Philip. *The Triumph of the Therapeutic: Uses of Faith after Freud.* New York: Harper & Row, 1966.

Ringe, Sharon H. *Jesus, Liberation, and the Biblical Jubilee: Image for Ethics and Christology.* Philadelphia: Fortress Press, 1985.

Ringgren, Helmer. *Israelite Religion.* Philadelphia: Fortress, 1966.

Robinson, H. Wheeler. *Inspiration and Revelation in the Old Testament.* Oxford: Clarendon Press, 1946.

Rowley, H. H. *The Servant of the Lord and Other Essays on the Old Testament.* 2d ed. Oxford: Basil Blackwell, 1965.

Russell, D. S. *Apocalyptic Ancient and Modern.* Philadelphia: Fortress Press, 1978.

————. *The Method and Message of Jewish Apocalyptic.* Philadelphia: Westminster Press, 1964.

Sanders, E. P. *Paul and Palestinian Judaism: A Comparison of Patterns of Religion.* Philadelphia: Fortress Press, 1977.

Schottroff, Luise and Stegemann, Wolfgang. *Jesus and the Hope of the Poor.* Maryknoll, N.Y.: Orbis Books, 1986.

Sölle, Dorothee. "Between Matter and Spirit: Why and in What Sense Must Theology Be Materialist?" *God of the Lowly: Socio-Historical Interpretations of the Bible,* ed. Willy Schottroff and Wolfgang Stegemann 86–102. Maryknoll, N.Y.: Orbis Books, 1984.

Stambaugh, John E. and Balch, David L. *The New Testament in Its Social Environment.* Philadelphia: Westminster Press, 1986.

Stegemann, Wolfgang. *The Gospel and the Poor*. Philadelphia: Fortress Press, 1984.

Stendahl, Krister. *Paul Among Jews and Gentiles*. Philadelphia: Fortress Press, 1976.

Tannehill, Robert C. *The Narrative Unity of Luke-Acts: A Literary Interpretation. Vol. 1: The Gospel According to Luke*. Philadelphia: Fortress Press, 1986.

Towner, W. Sibley. *Daniel*. Atlanta: John Knox Press, 1984.

von Rad, Gerhard. *Theology of the Old Testament*. 2 vols. New York: Harper & Row, 1965.

Walsh, J. P. M. *The Mighty from Their Thrones: Power in the Biblical Tradition*. Philadelpia: Fortress Press, 1987.

Wink, Walter. *Naming the Powers: The Language of Power in the New Testament*. Vol. 1: *The Powers*. Philadelphia: Fortress Press, 1984.

Yoder, John Howard. *The Politics of Jesus*. Grand Rapids: William B. Eerdmans, 1972.

Index

SCRIPTURE

Old Testament

Genesis
1–2	8–9, 83
1:25-30	8, 9
2:7, 17, 21-22	8, 83
4:25	12
12:1-3	61, 82
15:1-6	82
17:15—18:15	82

Exodus
3:7-8	24
3:7-12	12, 60
3:8	82
6:2-8	12
12	69
14	115
15:21	10
19:4-6	15, 61, 67
21–22	18
21:2	26
33:7-11	115

Leviticus
5:3	25
11:44, 45	25
12:2	25
15:1-15, 25	25
17–26	24–26
19:9-10	16
20:24	82
21:16-23	25
25	18
25:28	69
26:14-26	27

Numbers
5:2-4	25
12:9-10	27
14:8	82

Deuteronomy
5:1-5	61
5:6	15
6:18	82
15	18
15:3	26
18:18	61
23:24-25	17
24:1-4	50
26:16-19	61
26:18	15
26:19	69
28:15-24	27
34:10	61

Joshua
24	11

Judges
2:11-23	27
2:11	69
9	84
20:27	115

1 Samuel
2:6-7	27
8	84
11–12	21
16	84, 85
18:14	27

2 Samuel
7:11-17	85
23:5	85
11–12	70

1 Kings
19:14	70
19:15-18	85
21	70
22	70

2 Kings
9	70

Ezra
9–10	132

Nehemiah
5:1-13	19

Job
4:7-9	28
15:20	28
36:14-16	28
42:10	27

Psalms
2	85
2:7	20
9:9-10	24
10:17	23
10:18	24
18	85
20	85
21	85
22:1	53
25:16	24
34:6	23
35:10	24
45	85
68:6	24
69:32-33	23
72	85
72:1-4, 12-14	24
74:21	24
82:3-4	24
86:1-2, 7	24
89	85
98:9	24
99:4	24

107:41	23		56:7	22
109:31	23		58:6	33
110	85		61:1-2	19, 33
113:9	24			
116:6	24		*Jeremiah*	
132	85		5:26-27	20
140:12	23		7:5-11, 21-23	22
146:5-9	23		22:13-17	21
147:6	24		23:1-8	85
			27	138
Proverbs			31:31-34	86
3:33-35	27		33:14-16	85
6:6-15	28		34:8-22	19
21:17	28			
23:21	28		*Daniel*	
			7:13	87
Isaiah			11:31	87
2:1-4	86		12:12	87
7	138			
9:2-7	85		*Hosea*	
11:1-5	85		1:1	115
11:6-9	86			
40–55	10		*Amos*	
40:10-11	115		2:6-7	20
42:1-4	62, 63		4:1	20
42:5-9	22, 62		5:18-20	86
43:16-17	10		5:21-24	21
45:1-3	63			
49:1-6	62		*Jonah*	
49:1	62		4:2	22
49:6	62, 63, 71			
49:3	62		*Micah*	
50:4-10	63		2:1-2	20
50:4-9	62, 63		3:2-4	21
52:13—53:12	62, 63		4:1-4	86
53:7	42		5:2-4	85
54:11-13	86		6:6-8	21
54:13-14	86			
55:6-8	86			
55:12-13	86			
56:6-8	86			

Zechariah
9:9-10   85

New Testament

Matthew
2:5-6   89
5:3   34–35, 104
5:20   72
5:21—6:27   72
5:23-24   52
5:37   52
7:16   72
7:21-27   125
8:11   89
9:10-11   47
10   65
10:3   47
10:5   48
10:7   140
11:19   46
12:2   36
12:28   89
12:33   72
13:24-30   125
13:33   49
14:13-21   33
15:32-37   33
18:23-35   125
19:3-8   50
19:30   39
20:1-15   38
20:1-16   125
20:16   39
20:20-28   133
20:26-28   133
20:26   41
21:4-5   89
21:12-13   39
21:31   48
21:33-43   38

21:33-46   37
22:15-22   43
23:9   41
25:31-46   52, 72, 125
27:46   53

Mark
1:1, 11   53
1:16-20   32
1:21—2:12   32
1:30-31   32
1:39-41   46
1:40-44   40, 41, 46
2:1-12   46
2:15-16   41
2:15-17   46
2:23-28   38, 43
3:1-6   40, 46
3:11   54
3:34   41
5:5   36
5:7   54
5:9   36
5:24-34   40, 49
6:30-44   33
7:1-8   42
7:24-30,
   31-37   46
8:1-10   33, 46
8:38   89
9:8   53
10:2-9   50
10:30   39
10:35-45   42, 51, 133
11:15-17   39
11:18   53
12:1-12   37
12:13-17   43
12:30   127
12:41-44   39, 49
13   89

14:61	42		13:31-33	42
14:62-63	54		14:12-14	40
15:5	42		15:1-32	48
15:34	53		15:1	46, 48
15:39	53, 54		15:8-9	38, 49
			16:19-31	38
Luke			17:11-19	49, 139
1:52	43		18:9-14	48
1:68-74	43		18:11	47
2:25	43		18:18-23	38
2:36-38	46		18:35-43	139
2:38	43		19:1-10	38, 48
4:16-21	33, 39		19:2	47
4:18	104		19:43	43
4:35	36		19:45-48	39
5:12-14	50		19:47-48	53
6:17	37		20:9-18	37
6:20	34–35, 104		20:20-26	43
7:11	50		22:24-27	133
7:18-23	33, 39		23:40-43	50
7:34	46		24:21	43
7:36-50	36, 49, 139		24:27	89
7:37-50	48, 50		24:48-49	66
7:38	46			
8:1-3	38, 41, 50		*John*	
8:40	50		1:1	115
9:10-17	33		1:1-18	54, 144
9:42	36		1:14	115, 116
9:51-56	49		1:18	31
10	65		2:13-17	39
10:4	71		3:16	64, 65, 144
10:9	65, 140		4:1-42	48, 49
10:17-20	66		4:7-26	41
10:29-37	49		5:42-47	64
10:30-37	41		6:1-13	33
10:38-42	49		6:38-44	64
11:2	51		7:49	36
12:13-21	38		8:18	64
13:1-5	28, 35		8:26	64
13:20-21	49		9:1-4	28, 35
13:30	39		10:36	64

11	32, 50	15:25-28	73
12	50		
14:27	144	*1 Corinthians*	
15:9	65	2:8	90
15:26-27	115	5:7	10
17	64, 75	12:1	75
20:1-18	50	12:12-31	145
20:10-23	64, 66, 143–45	12:13	73, 132
		13:13	125
Acts		15	89–90
2:1-40	66	16:1-4	73
2:44-45	73		
2:47	73	*2 Corinthians*	
3:1-10	66	1–9	138
3:12-26	66	2:12	75
3:19	66	3:17	129
4:4	66	5:16-17	113
4:14	67	5:21	54
5:1-6	73	8–9	73
6:1-7	73, 138		
8:7	67	*Galatians*	
8:26-35	89	2	124, 132
10:34	74	2:10	73
10:38	67	2:15-16	74
15:36-41	138	3:13	54
28:10	67	3:23-29	130
		3:28	73, 127, 132
Romans		4:4	64
3:19-26	74	4:6	64
3:21	129	4:16	122
3:28	122	5:1	129
6	124	5:6	124
8:3	64		
9–11	132	*Ephesians*	
10:8	115	2:14-15	76
12:1	124	6:8	73
12:2	113		
12:3-8	145	*Philippians*	
13	92	2:5-11	54
15	124		

Colossians
3:10   132
3:11   73

1 Thessalonians
3:13   75
4:7   75
4:15-18   89

Hebrews
12:10   75
12:14   75

James
1:9-11   75
1:22   75
1:27   75
2:1-7   132
2:1-9   75
2:5   75
2:14-26   75

2:17, 22   125
4:6, 10   75
5:14-15   75

1 Peter
1:23-25   73
2:13-15   92

1 John
4:16   55
4:18   141
4:19   144

Revelation
1:9   91
5:12   93
13   91
17:14   93
18:1-19   93
20   91
21–22   90, 92

SUBJECTS

Abba, 41, 51
Abraham, 61
Accomplishment, 111
Acts of the Apostles, 66–67,
    72–73, 115, 135, 138
Advocacy, 137
    advocate, 16–19, 23, 50
Agapē, 55
Agency/Agent, 13, 60–68,
    144–45
    See envoy
AIDS, 67, 111, 137
Alternative community, 68–78,
    117
Amos, 20, 21
Ananias and Sapphira, 73

Anointed, 20, 63
    anointing, 84
    See Messiah
'Apiru, 11, 69
Apocalyptic, 86, 87–88, 91
Ascetic, 105
Associations, Jesus', 46–50, 51
Authorization, 145

Baalim, 69
Barnabas, 138
Beatitudes, 34–35, 104

Canaan, 69, 82, 115
Charity, 108–9, 118
Cleanness, ritual, 25, 45

Community, 3, 59–60, 61–64,
  67–78, 105–7, 113–14,
  117, 138
Compassion, 13
Complexity of social problems,
  107–8, 134–35
Consciousness, 146–47
  popular, 99–118
  alternative consciousness,
    114, 117, 118
  prophetic consciousness, 114
  royal consciousness, 70, 84,
    114
Controversy, 136–38
Corporatism, 105–7
  See community
Counter–images, 24–29, 35, 55
Counterculture, 41, 68
Covenant, 14–15, 21, 61, 69
  covenant code, 18
Creation, 8–9, 144
  Creator, 9, 14
Cross, 52–55
Cyrus, 63

Daniel, 87–88
David, 21, 70, 84–85
Davidic dynasty, 85
Day of the Lord, 86
Death, 90
  Jesus', 52–55, 144
Dereliction, cry of, 53
Despair, 135
Deutero–Isaiah, 10, 22
Deuteronomic Code, 18

Economic welfare, 37–39
Election, divine, 15
Elijah, 69–70
Elisha, 70
Emotional health, 35–37

Emperor, 43
  emperor cult, 91
Empowerment, 80–81, 107–8,
  133, 135
  See power
Environment, 19
Envoy, 64, 147
Eschatology, 79–94
Ethnicity, 73–74
Evangelism and social ministry,
  140–41
Evil, 87, 90–91, 92–93
Exclusivism, 44–46, 71, 102
  exclusion, 22–23, 26
Exodus, 9–15, 17, 18, 60–61,
  82
Exorcism, 36, 40, 139
Experts, 62, 80, 108, 134
Ezra, Book of, 132

Faith
  and fatalism, 135–36
  and works, 122–30
Fatalism, 135–36
Fear, 121–41, 146
  justification, 127–30
  of failure, 127–30
  of change, 131–32
  practical fears, 130–41
  theological, 122–30
  works righteousness, 123–27
Freedom, 74, 77, 83, 87, 92,
  101, 109, 112, 129–30,
  142
Future,
  in Old Testament, 81–88
  in New Testament, 88–94
  in Paul, 89–91
  in prophets, 83–88
  in Revelation, 91–94
  in Torah, 81–83

God
  advocate of the poor, 16–17
  advocate of justice, 17–19
  care for all persons, 44–51
  care for the whole person,
    32–44
  identified with suffering,
    51–55
  images of, 7–8
  liberator, 10–11
  passionate, 11–13
  of the covenant and law,
    14–19
  of creation, 8–9
  of exclusion, 24–26
  of the exodus, 9–14
  of the psalmists, 23–24
  of the prophets, 19–23
Gospel, 116, 122, 123, 130,
    137, 145
Grace, 122, 126, 129

Habits of the Heart, 101–2
Healing, 66–67, 139
  Jesus' healing, 32–33, 40
Holiness, 25, 45, 75
Holiness Code, 24–25
Holism, 103–5, 118, 146
Holy Spirit, 66, 115, 135, 144,
    145
Homogeneity, 131–32
Hope, 80
Humanitarianism, ix–x
Hunger, 33, 146

Image, 7–8, 31–32
Incarnation, 64, 116, 144, 145
Inclusiveness, 22–23, 44, 86,
    104, 115
  inclusivism, 87
  inclusivism, Jesus', 46–51

Individualism, 101, 102, 105–7,
    110, 126
Injustice, 19, 86, 88, 103
  unjust, 20
  See justice
Israel, 61, 69, 89, 114

James, 75, 125, 132
Jeremiah, 20, 21, 22, 138
John, Gospel of, 48, 49, 50,
    75–76, 143–45
  evangelist, 54, 64–65
John of Patmos, 81, 91–94
Jonah, 22
Jubilee year, 18–19
Justice, 17–19, 21, 23–24, 69,
    72, 74, 77, 85, 86, 87, 101,
    108–9, 118
  just, 20–21,
Justification by faith, 74,
    122–30, 144
Justification fear, 127–30

Kindness, ix–x
Kingdom of God, 65, 80, 89

Land, 82–83, 114
Lamb, 93
Law, 14–19, 69, 86, 114
  See Torah
Liberation, 13–14, 61, 77, 84,
    92, 111–12
  expense of, 13–14
  liberator, 10–11, 17, 18, 23,
    69
Luke, gospel of, 48, 49–50
  evangelist, 33–34, 43, 50

Maccabees, 87
Mark, gospel of, 32, 53–54

Materiality, 9, 83
material reality, 8–9
Matthew, Gospel of, 34, 72, 89, 125
Messiah, 89
messianic passages, 85
Metaphor, 8, 41
Micah, 20, 21
Micaiah, 70
Minority(ies), 11, 13–14
Mission, 2–3, 140–41, 143–47
Monarchy, 20, 83–86
Moses, 10–13, 60–61, 66, 69, 115

Narrative, 117
Nathan, 21, 70
Need, physical, 32–35, 52, 73
Networking, 134

Obedience, 15
Oppression, 15, 69, 84, 86, 88, 92
oppressive, 11
oppressor(s), 13–14
oppressed, 14, 17

Parables, 37, 38, 47–48, 49
Passion, of God, 11
Passover, 10
Paul, 54, 73–74, 89–91, 113, 115, 124–25, 127, 129, 132, 138, 145
Parousia, 89
Passivity, 80
Peace, 86, 126–27, 137, 143–45
Peter, 66, 74
Philistines, 84
Pietistic, 104
Plagues, 13
Pluralism, 132–33

Political,
leaders, 20–21, 86
welfare, 42–43, 85
system, 92
Possessions, 38
Poverty, 19, 108
poor, 16–17, 18, 23–24, 37–39, 103
Power, 133, 145
powerlessness, 107–8
powers, cosmic, 90–91, 92
See empowerment
Promise, 81–83
promise–fulfillment, 63, 81–94
Property,
real estate, 18
redistribution, 19
communal, 73
Prophet(s), 10, 19–22, 83–88, 114, 138
prophetic literature, 62, 86–87
prophetic movement, 70
Prostitutes, 48
Psalms, 23–24
royal, 85–86
Public life, 102

Qumran, 45

Racism, 91
racial discrimination, 101
Responsibility, 17, 21, 65
responsible, 20
Resurrection, 89–90
Retribution, divine, 26–28
Retribution ethic, 27–28
Revelation, Book of, 91–94
Righteousness, 15, 72, 85, 125, 129

Risk, 139–40

Sabbatical year, 18–19, 47
Sacraments, 10, 116
Samaritans, 41, 48–49
Samuel, 84
Saul, 85
Scroll of the Rule, 45
Sectarian, 76
Self–interest, 106
Servant of the Lord, 62–63,
    70–71, 114
Servanthood, 133
Setting, of Jesus' ministry,
    44–46
Seventy, mission of, 65–66
Shelter, 17
Sinners, 46, 129
Slavery, 82
    slave(s), 18
    enslavement, 111–12
Social ministry and evangelism,
    140–41
Society,
    social class, 11, 40–41
    social morality, 21–22,
    social relationships, 20, 126
    social solidarity, 100
    social welfare, 39–42
Social science, 106
Spiritual, 2
    spiritual reality, 9
    spiritualization, 34, 103–5
Stranger, 18
Success, 101, 128, 130

Suffering, 51–55, 63, 71, 93,
    103, 144
    vicarious, 63
Tax collectors, 46–48
Taxation, 46–47
Teaching, 117, 146
Temple cleansing, 39, 53
Theism, moral, 16
Torah, 19, 83, 124
    See law
Transformation, 99–118, 146

Unemployment, 107
Unrighteousness, 21
    See righteousness

Values, 68, 72, 77

Welfare,
    economic, 37–39
    emotional, 35–37
    physical, 32–35
    political, 42–43
    social, 39–42
    system, 17
Women, 13–14, 49–50, 74,
    103, 109
Work ethic, 110, 122
Works righteousness, 123–27
Worship, 21–22
Worth, achieved and intrinsic,
    109–11, 139

Yadah, 12
Yahweh, 11, 115

NT
O.T
nang
Prophets
preaching
Exegetical Methods
Greek
#1

cm#2
1 Sue
2. Ethics
cm #3
Pastoral Care
2 CPE —
2 found Place
Systemic Theo
Independent Study

Printed in the United States
1356300001B/283-321